Career
Distinction

Career Distinction

Stand Out by Building Your Brand

William Arruda
Kirsten Dixson

John Wiley & Sons, Inc.

Copyright © 2007 by William Arruda and Kirsten Dixson. All rights reserved.

Published by John Wiley & Sons, Inc., Hoboken, New Jersey.
Published simultaneously in Canada.

Wiley Bicentennial Logo: Richard J. Pacifico

No part of this publication may be reproduced, stored in a retrieval system, or transmitted in any form or by any means, electronic, mechanical, photocopying, recording, scanning, or otherwise, except as permitted under Section 107 or 108 of the 1976 United States Copyright Act, without either the prior written permission of the Publisher, or authorization through payment of the appropriate per-copy fee to the Copyright Clearance Center, Inc., 222 Rosewood Drive, Danvers, MA 01923, (978) 750-8400, fax (978) 646-8600, or on the web at www.copyright.com. Requests to the Publisher for permission should be addressed to the Permissions Department, John Wiley & Sons, Inc., 111 River Street, Hoboken, NJ 07030, (201) 748-6011, fax (201) 748-6008, or online at http://www.wiley.com/go/permissions.

Limit of Liability/Disclaimer of Warranty: While the publisher and author have used their best efforts in preparing this book, they make no representations or warranties with respect to the accuracy or completeness of the contents of this book and specifically disclaim any implied warranties of merchantability or fitness for a particular purpose. No warranty may be created or extended by sales representatives or written sales materials. The advice and strategies contained herein may not be suitable for your situation. You should consult with a professional where appropriate. Neither the publisher nor author shall be liable for any loss of profit or any other commercial damages, including but not limited to special, incidental, consequential, or other damages.

For general information on our other products and services or for technical support, please contact our Customer Care Department within the United States at (800) 762-2974, outside the United States at (317) 572-3993 or fax (317) 572-4002.

Wiley also publishes its books in a variety of electronic formats. Some content that appears in print may not be available in electronic books. For more information about Wiley products, visit our website at www.wiley.com.

Library of Congress Cataloging-in-Publication Data:

Arruda, William, 1961–
    Career distinction : stand out by building your brand / William Arruda,
Kirsten Dixson.
        p.   cm.
    Includes index.
    ISBN-13: 978-0-470-12818-3 (cloth)
    1. Career development.   2. Success in business.   3. Professions—Marketing.
I. Dixson, Kirsten, 1968–   II. Title.
    HF5381.A828   2007
    650.14—dc22
                                                          2006039541

Printed in the United States of America.

10 9 8 7 6 5 4 3 2

Contents

STEP THREE

EXUDE—MANAGE YOUR BRAND ENVIRONMENT

Foreword

I have lived and breathed career management for over 30 years, and in that time I have seen seismic changes in the world of work and consequently in the field of career management. The biggest shocks have all come in the past 10 years. The coming of the Information Age, and the tsunami of the Internet engulfing our daily lives, has rendered most beliefs about career management, for those who ever held any, obsolete.

Becoming credible and visible in your career is more than just the reward of doing a good job; it is the result of working consistently over the years to make a difference to those you serve and to those with whom you work. The more you work toward credibility and visibility in your profession, the quicker you enter that inner circle—in your department, in your company, and ultimately in your industry. One of the many rewards for this effort is that you get to know and be known by the most committed and best connected in your profession. That is how I got to know William Arruda and Kirsten Dixson. They have become valuable members of the leadership community on career management thought.

One thing that links the most successful professionals at all levels is that they take a proactive approach to managing their careers. People who are ahead of the game don't wait for a career emergency to activate their network or update their resume. As Arruda and Dixson explain, you have to make career management a habit. Their innovative, step-by-step approach focuses on personal branding—a new concept for most of us that is largely misrepresented in the media. In this book, Arruda and Dixson dispel the myths and demonstrate that if you get personal branding right, you will attract your ideal opportunities rather than having to seek them out. Like them, you can increase the success and enjoyment that you bring to your work by making the most of who you really are.

The future is bright for those who are able to manage their careers the way that companies manage their businesses. Like companies, people must be incredibly clear about what they uniquely offer and who benefits from it. People must engage in ongoing communication activities to keep their personal brands in the forefront. And they must ensure that everything that they do delivers on their brand promise.

Arruda and Dixson are two pioneers in building and managing online identity; in fact, they improved mine. What they do is becoming more and more vital as we are all Googled before meetings and interviews.

Adopting the *Career Distinction* mindset and integrating the ideas from this book into your career strategy will have a positive impact on your career. Listen to what Arruda and Dixson have to say; it could make a real difference in your professional life.

MARTIN YATE
Author of *Knock 'em Dead: The Ultimate Job Search Guide*

Preface

In the new world of work, your reputation is the only accepted currency. Whether you are looking to move up the corporate ladder in your current organization, find a position at another company, make a major career change, or start your own enterprise, you will no longer be hunting for your next role. Instead, opportunities will come to you. Colleagues, hiring managers, clients, and recruiters will use search engines like Google as well as social and professional networks to find out about you and reach you. To thrive in this new environment, you must identify your personal assets and clearly communicate your unique promise of value. Your credibility and visibility will drive demand for your services. You must use *who* you are to affect *how* you earn. That's where *Career Distinction: Stand Out by Building Your Brand* comes in.

This definitive step-by-step guide enables you to determine how others perceive you, reshape those perceptions to achieve your goals, and communicate your message about your personal brand clearly and consistently. In this book, you learn how to become the "must-have" professional—by being yourself. We demonstrate the power that comes with being yourself by providing examples of people (some names have been changed for privacy) just like you who have achieved professional success and fulfillment by living their personal brands. But before we introduce you to these fascinating people, let us introduce ourselves.

Who are we, and why did we join forces to write this book? William is the perfect example of someone who initially had no career strategy whatsoever. When he was deciding on a major in college, he chose to go into engineering. He selected this discipline because he knew he would find it difficult, and he thought university had to be hard. And it was. He was thankful for the electives and humanities courses that kept his grade point average in an acceptable range. William had no awareness of his own passions or motivations—yet they were clear to those around him. For example, he had a deep interest in advertising from a young age. Over the years, he built up a large collection of TV advertisements on VHS and watched television more for the commercials than for the programs. In his words:

> After graduating from school, I took on many marketing tasks while a consultant at KMPG and then officially moved into marketing in the information technology sector. I felt at ease there—motivated, energized. But it wasn't until I had the incredible opportunity to manage the rebranding effort for Primark—a financial services company—that I realized my passion for branding. I had always been an ambassador of my favorite brands—Apple, Starbucks, W Hotels, Moulton Brown. With this project, I was able to learn about and apply the principles of branding for myself.
>
> As I progressed in my career, I started to manage more and more people and discovered my other passion—empowering and mentoring others. I saw the power of helping people discover their talents, advance their careers, and reach their potential.
>
> Then, something amazing happened. It was July 1997. I was working for Lotus in Cambridge, MA (the best company I ever worked for), and was busily writing a report. I needed a break, so I went out to my assistant's desk and saw the new issue of *Fast Company*. I took the magazine outside, sat on a bench near the Charles River, and read the cover story, "The Brand Called You," by Tom Peters. It was like all the planets aligned for me. That article cemented the connection between my two great passions: branding and people. In reading that article, I took my initial step toward launching the first global personal branding company.
>
> With a vision of entrepreneurship shining in my mind, I moved to London and then to Paris to manage the Lotus brand in

Europe. Finally, in 2001, while in my office at La Defense in Paris, I decided it was time to launch Reach. The rest is history.

Of course, 2001 wasn't the best year to start a company, so it was a rocky start. And back then, no one had heard of personal branding—let alone wanted to spend any money on it. But, six years later, my only regret is that I didn't launch the business sooner.

My career now focuses exclusively on the human side of branding. I work with professionals and entrepreneurs to help them use their personal brands to stand out and expand their success. I assist senior leaders in building their executive brands so they can make indelible marks on their organizations. And I deliver keynotes and workshops for forward-thinking organizations that want to get the best from their talent by helping employees unearth and leverage their unique value.

So I have found my niche and have increased my professional fulfillment. I live my personal brand every day. It is now my mission to help others to do the same.

What makes you unique, makes you successful.

—William Arruda

Now we introduce you to Kirsten. William met Kirsten when she joined the initial session of the Reach Personal Branding Certification program. In fact, she was the first person to register. He knew instantly that she was an innovator. She absorbed the Reach personal branding methodology as if it were in her DNA. There were times during the program when William thought Kirsten was more excited about the material than even he was. As Kirsten relates it:

Like William, I had no real plan for my career. I wasn't sure how to turn my disparate interests in theatre, international travel, foreign languages, and writing into a career that would satisfy my creative and entrepreneurial spirit. I transferred to Vassar College in my sophomore year and immediately had to choose a major in a new school. Because I had enjoyed acting, I thought "why not be a drama major?" Somehow, it made sense at the time, even though I knew that I would never be a professional actor. In the summer between my junior and senior years, I taught English in Thailand through AFS. I came back wishing that I had been an international studies major, but it was too late to switch and still graduate on the four-year plan.

As I entered the real world and had to search for my first nonsummer job, I was filled with unrealistic expectations about how I'd begin my career and took the first offer I got. Out of character, I worked in sales management support for a retail computer chain where I was fortunate to gain a lot of my early technology knowledge. After a shocking layoff, I found my way to the more tumultuous world of advertising.

I was working on the Peugeot Motors of America account when Peugeot decided not to sell cars in the United States. Then I worked on a new business pitch for Mazda: The agency I worked for won the account, and then the car was not introduced. I was laid off again. This time, I was sent to outplacement where I discovered that there was an entire industry devoted to helping me with my career. I then moved to Los Angeles (for love) and switched to the seemingly more stable "client side" of marketing. Among other things, I facilitated the international brand licensing program for Kahlúa. (I should also mention that amid these transitions, I held some long-term freelance assignments that gave me an insider's view of companies in a variety of industries.) When the parent company reorganized, I opted for a package and moved back to New York. Before I left, I went to outplacement again.

I took part in a group seminar led by a particularly effective trainer who was talking about the concept of Me Inc.—long before it was mainstream. Right then and there, I decided that I wanted her job. In that moment, I realized that I could finally be in control of my own destiny and use my strengths and experience to help others do the same. I enrolled in NYU's Adult Career Planning and Development program, and I was on my way to discovering my true calling. After my first daughter was born,

I resigned from my position at a human resources consulting firm and launched a career marketing service that I sold a few years ago. Although I mostly specialized in working with career changers, I helped hundreds of professionals at all levels in a wide variety of industries, and I really didn't yet have a personal brand.

> *Building your personal brand online gets you noticed in the real world.*
>
> —Kirsten Dixson

Now, back to William to explain how we began our collaboration:

One day, Kirsten sent me an e-mail asking if we could meet in person. (The certification program was delivered through teleseminars.) We met face-to-face for the first time in Boston before she was scheduled to review resumes at a Women for Hire expo. Kirsten told me about her plans to launch Brandego® (pronounced brand-eh-go)—a consultancy for executives and solopreneurs to build their brands online—and asked me to be involved. This was the perfect business for Kirsten. She is future focused and anticipated the need for people to manage their online identities before the term *ego-surfing* even existed.

At the same time, I was looking to launch an e-learning product, the Reach Branding Club, that would give professionals everything they need to brand themselves at their own pace and for an affordable fee. Many people had come to me looking for brand coaching but weren't able to or didn't want to pay my hourly fees. I had the intellectual property—the content and methodology—and I needed to partner with someone who could find the most innovative and interesting, yet simple, way of delivering the material. There was only one person I could think of.

Kirsten is perhaps the biggest believer in the Reach methodology (okay, maybe the second). She uses it with every one of her clients. It's integrated into her offerings at Brandego, and she talks about it with everyone she meets. Combine this with her passion for leveraging the Internet for career success, and you have the perfect coauthor for this book.

William started writing this book in 2001 with his then coauthor, Andrea O'Neill (a bright, accomplished branding and marketing expert). At the time, the book was titled *Bulletproof Your Career*—which reflected the post-Internet bubble economy where layoffs were the norm and job security was a pipe dream. When Andrea decided the book did not fit into her future plans, William left the files on the Reach server until he saw many books being published about personal branding—and noticed that none of them dealt with the future of work. Not a single author of these books described the shift in mindset necessary to succeed in the changing economy. He felt inspired to begin writing again. Having seen the value of working with a coauthor, he asked Kirsten to join him. And you're holding the result in your hands. Writing this book has been nothing short of life changing for us. We hope you take away from it a little of the inspiration we have felt in writing it.

In this book, we share with you the forward-thinking methods for standing out from your competitors and peers that we have helped our clients to adopt. With the companion *Career Distinction Workbook* and access to the 360°Reach personal brand assessment (both available at www.careerdistinction.com/workbook), you have all the tools you need to transform your approach to career management for an enduring and rewarding career.

Acknowledgments

I would like to thank my parents, Joe and Barbara; and my sisters, Doreen and Beverly, for their constant and unconditional love and support. I would also like to thank Andrea O'Neill, who contributed her creativity and writing to the original manuscript, and Kirsten Dixson—the perfect business and writing partner—whose energy and drive helped make this book and the Reach Branding Club a reality. I would also like to express heart-felt gratitude to Joao Rocco, Susan Gladwin, Suzanne Tanner-Meisel, Suzette Fraser, Nancy Preston, Hans Nystrom, and "la Famille" in Paris for their friendship, inspiration, and encouragement. Finally, I would like to recognize Paul Copcutt and the 150+ Reach-Certified Personal Branding Strategists who span the globe and are committed to using the Reach personal branding methodology to enhance the lives and careers of their clients.

W. A.

Most importantly, I want to thank William Arruda for asking me to write this book with him. The gratitude that I have for everything that I've learned from William and all the ways that he has accelerated my career is beyond words. I would also like to express my deepest appreciation to:

> Brian Wu, without whom there would not be Brandego. Brian's vast talent and wisdom has elevated every project on which we've collaborated.

Wendy Enelow for initially recognizing that career technology should be my niche.

My husband, Chris, for his support in fulfilling my dreams and being a great father to Abby and Cate.

My mom for consistently believing that I could do anything, her sacrifices on our behalf, and making sure that I could communicate well.

My dad for instilling his entrepreneurial spirit in me and for a "launch in and learn as you go approach" that has served me well.

Nathan for teaching me to make each day count.

K. D.

Together we would like to thank Wendy Enelow for reviewing our book proposal and encouraging us to go for it; Jennifer Sneirson Kun and Brian Wu for creating images for this book; L. Michelle Tullier for connecting us with our publisher; Laurie Johnson for her editing expertise; and the Reach Strategists whose contributions are in the book: Kim Batson, Paul Copcutt, and Deb Dib.

Chapter 1

Understand the Future of Work

In this chapter, you will learn:

- The factors that are impacting our careers
- What employers are really looking for

To help you make the most of this book, let us set the scene for you and pose a question: What is happening in the world of work, and how can you succeed in this new paradigm?

Change Is the Only Constant

The accelerating retirement of the baby boomers and worsening shortage of knowledge workers are just a few of the trends reshaping the labor market and making personal branding more crucial than ever. To put the advice in this book into context, consider the following additional changes you can expect in the employment landscape of the new millennium.

> *Change is the law of life. And those who look only to the past or present are certain to miss the future.*
>
> —John F. Kennedy, 35th President
> of the United States

Shrinking Job Tenure

In both prosperous *and* challenging economic times, the duration of job tenure decreases. During periods of economic growth, job hunting and job hopping intensifies. And, during economic recessions, downsizing further shrinks job tenure. Consider these facts:

- According to the U.S. Department of Labor, over the past few decades, the average length of time a person stays in a job in every sector of private business has decreased.[1] Today, employees change their jobs every two years, their companies every three, and their industries every four.

- A 2005 ExecuNet survey revealed that corporate leaders are changing companies every 3.6 years, down from 4.1 years in 2002.[2] For some occupations, the expected average tenure is even shorter. Take chief marketing officers: At the world's top-100 branded companies, CMO tenure is just under two years, according to a 2004 Spencer Stuart survey.[3] Why the revolving door? CMOs are now accountable for return on investment (ROI).

- In a project-based world, the new loyalty is to the project at hand. If the project doesn't deliver results that directly boost the bottom line, the typical organization will cancel it—along with team members' employment contracts. This is not a secret to most career-minded professionals: A 2006 Pew study revealed that 62 percent of Americans believe that there is less job security today than there was 20 or 30 years ago.[4]

In this dynamic environment, the time you have to make your mark is reduced. You must be crystal clear about the value you bring to your organization and the specific project. You must deliver that value consistently and, at the same time, be prepared for changes to your assignment or employer. The first 100-day plan, once reserved for CEOs, is something you need to bring to every new assignment.

Blurred Boundaries between Work and Personal Life

The BlackBerry, ubiquitous Wi-Fi, and mobile phones have created a "work anytime, anywhere" world. This blurring of boundaries between professional and personal life will only increase as being in the office becomes less and less necessary for knowledge workers. Again, the facts and figures say it all:

- With the exception of France (where the work week has been reduced), the number of hours we work each week has increased. In 1969, couples in the United States, aged 25 to 54, worked a combined 56 hours per week. By the year 2000, they were working nearly 70 hours.[5]

- Hotels, airports, Starbucks, and cafés have become Wi-Fi zones, making it easy for people to work from any location. Entire cities, like Philadelphia and San Jose are becoming "Wi-Fied." And you can expect Wi-Fi on aircraft and in many public places in the coming years. Companies are starting to expect an "always-on" attitude from employees.

As you spend more time working from remote locations, your visibility around the office will decrease despite the increase in work hours. Your personal brand must be powerful enough to impact colleagues and managers even when you are not physically present. This freedom allows you to work from anywhere at times that are convenient for you; but you now have to ensure that you're communicating your value with every e-mail and every phone call. And if you are going to be on the job all the time, you'll want to increase the fulfillment you gain from your work, aligning it with your values and passions.

This book is a testament to the virtual project team. The authors have only been in the same city at the same time twice during the writing of the book. We have never met our editor in person, nor have we met in person with our graphic designers who created the images for the book. Most of William's words were written while on a plane or in an airport lounge. Yet, with an electronic project management system, Wi-Fi, and Skype, we put this book together on a short schedule.

Accelerating Organizational Change

Under increasing pressure from Wall Street to grow revenue and profits, companies are continuously extending into new business areas, expanding internationally, merging with and acquiring other entities, outsourcing work, and rethinking their products and services. Consider these trends:

- Companies continue to leverage technology to ensure that information flows where it is needed. Use of technology renders geographic boundaries less important, making all organizations global and all businesses e-businesses.
- Globalization and technology advances are forcing companies to develop more fluid and complex organizational structures characterized by cross-organizational networking, alliances, and outsourcing of noncore activities to specialized agencies.
- Regulations such as the Sarbanes-Oxley Act are creating jobs in finance and corporate law, while IT jobs are being handled offshore.
- More work is done in the United States by fewer people, as evidenced by the rise in productivity. Information technology and the pressure on companies to increase shareholder value through economies of scale have driven this productivity increase.

Just when you understand how things are working in your current organization, they are likely to change. The rate of change is increasing and many external factors that are beyond your control impact how you work. The burgeoning flexibility of organizational structures increased the options for how your job can be accomplished. And the people competing for your job are no longer the people in your city; they are the people in the next city, state, and even country. Likewise, you will have the opportunity to work on projects that are located in Paris even if you are living in Peoria. Those who embrace change and accept it as a constant will reap the benefits of this ever-changing environment.

Employees' Growing Mobility

The shift from guaranteed company-sponsored pensions to employee self-managed retirement plans has enabled employees to be more mobile. You no longer have to be tied to a job that you don't like until you turn 65. It's been a long time since we've encountered someone who even wanted to work for the same company for his or her entire career. In addition, professionals alternate between working for organizations and working for themselves. Thus, they need to develop and implement ongoing personal marketing plans to be constantly prepared for their next assignment, all while making strong contributions to their current employer or clients.

Standing still is not an option. Constant reorganization means constant disruption in the workforce—meaning that employees at all levels must continually manage their own careers rather than waiting for their employers to do so. You can't expect things to remain static, nor can you entirely predict the future. So, the only way to ensure that you achieve the career of your dreams is to build demand for your unique offerings. This may sound daunting, but in fact it is the opposite. It gives you the opportunity to profit from your work both financially and personally. It enables you to firmly grip the reins of your career and direct your energy toward your goals.

What Employers Really Want

Just like you, employers want to stay ahead of the competition. They want customers to see their products as different from—and better than—all the other options out there in the market. And they want to command the highest possible prices for their offerings. They crave a creative workforce comprising professionals and leaders who can deliver innovative solutions that meet consumers' most pressing needs. Innovation requires creativity—which in turn derives from a diverse workforce of individuals who are maximizing their unique strengths.

The importance of diversity will continue to expand down to the individual level. Conformity is the enemy of innovation. So you will have the opportunity to be yourself and to succeed because of it. When you are just one of many others with similar skills and abilities, you don't contribute to the diversity your organization needs to generate creative, innovative ideas. Instead, you become a commodity. And people don't get excited about commodities. Ever hear someone say, "I love crude oil" or "I love pork bellies"? Being a "Me-Too" executive, manager, or professional doesn't cut it in the new world of work. Our message: Be yourself!

Our original plan for this book was to offer several chapters of detailed analysis showing how the employment model has shifted in order to demonstrate why you must change your career-management strategy. Then, we recognized that savvy careerists are well aware—sometimes painfully—that the days of corporate uniforms and pension plans are long gone. The standard career-management tools of the past have become less potent. Indeed, it has become so commonplace for people's resumes to acknowledge layoffs and gaps that any associated stigma has virtually evaporated.

On an intellectual level, you probably know that you should be managing your career just as you would your own business. After all, the idea of Me Inc. has been around for more than 10 years. However, in our career and personal branding practices, we consistently encounter business professionals who have not internalized this concept enough to actually change their career-management *behaviors*. Some of these individuals understand that they should think and act differently, but they aren't sure which career-management tools and techniques are most effective. Others simply haven't had to start managing their careers differently: They've advanced easily through referrals from their network, and opportunity after opportunity has just appeared at their feet. Still others aren't technology-savvy. For example, a person who hasn't had to look for a job in the past five years might be unsure of how to use the Internet effectively in a search for new opportunities. Inexperience about online job hunting abounds because too many people wrongly assume that they can just post their resume on a job board and then sit back and wait for the perfect opportunity to present itself.

KEITH DENNY, BUSINESS DIRECTOR, FOOTWEAR INDUSTRY

Keith Denny's story is typical: Keith enjoyed a stellar, progressively responsible career at Nike Inc. after graduating from college. He managed the inaugural Niketown store and worked his way up to director of the $350 million custom-footwear business. Then he was recruited by a New England-based global outdoor apparel company, moved his family across the country, and became vice president of Global Brand Management for its most profitable category. For 18 solid years, Keith enjoyed successive promotions because his strong industry contacts knew his reputation for excellence and his talent for developing his people. Keith never had to look for a job or angle for a promotion. Only once did he ever prepare a resume—and that was when he was recruited away from Nike.

After three years with Keith's new company, the composition and aims of the company's management team changed. Keith saw the warning signs that his job was on the line. For the first time, he began working with a career coach to plan his long-term objectives and chart his next steps. As a man in his middle years, Keith strongly desired more work-life balance and a greater sense of fulfillment from his work. Although his company was well known for its community service initiatives, Keith rarely felt that he had the time to participate in them. As a result, he felt unfulfilled by his role.

In conversations with his coach, he realized that he wasn't up-to-date on current job-search methods, because he had never had to use them. An introvert, Keith also felt uncomfortable with networking and touting his qualifications. He and his coach had just begun work on his resume the day before Keith was summoned to HR, where he learned that he was about to be laid off. Although Keith had taken some tentative steps in the right direction, he wasn't nearly prepared to launch a strategic job search.

New World of Work—New Opportunity

In today's new world of work, the pace is increasingly blistering and the competition constantly stiffening. Yet, the confluence of social, technological, and economic forces that have transformed the business landscape presents you with tremendous new opportunities. By opening your eyes to what's happening in the corporate world, you boost your chances of identifying the kinds of opportunities that most appeal to you. And you position yourself to seize those opportunities by making sure that those around you know precisely what you have to offer.

> *Too many people are thinking of security instead of opportunity. They seem more afraid of life than death.*
> —James F. Byrnes, U.S. jurist and politician

Notes

1. U.S. Department of Labor, *Asian Pacific American Federal Career Guide*, May 10, 2006, www.dol.gov/_sec_federal_career_guide .pdf.

2. ExecuNet Press Release, "Average Executive Tenure Less than Four Years," June 15, 2005, http://www.execunet.com /m_releases_content.cfm?id=3096.

3. Greg Welch, "CMO Tenure: Slowing Down the Revolving Door," July 2004, http://www.spencerstuart.com/research/articles/744.

4. Ruy Teixeira, "What the Public Really Wants on Jobs and the Economy," October 26, 2006, http://www.americanprogress.org /issues/2006/10/public_wants.html.

5. U.S. Bureau of Labor Statistics, "Working in the 21st Century," http://www.bls.gov/opub/working/page17b.htm.

Chapter 2

Adopt the Career Distinction Mindset

In this chapter, you will learn:

- The four principles of the *Career Distinction* mindset
- The importance of continuous career management

To succeed and find fulfillment in your work in this dynamic age, you must change the way you think about your career and you must treat career management as an ongoing activity. Creating your personal brand helps you do all of this—with the ultimate goal of distinguishing yourself for career success. In this book, we present a personal branding road map that we call 1-2-3 Success! (developed by Reach and proven with thousands of executives). Building your personal brand takes time—but it is also highly worthwhile. If you invest in the process now, things will get easier later. But before you jump into the process, let's take a closer look at the mindset you must adopt in order to apply 1-2-3 Success! to managing your career. We call this mindset *Career Distinction*. Adopt the *Career Distinction* mindset, follow the principles, and get ready to grab hold of your future.

Principle 1   Stand Out: Stand for Something

As you saw in Chapter 1, just doing your job, and even doing it well, is no longer enough. *Loyalty* and *longevity* were the watchwords of an earlier day. You saw this reflected in the TV programs of the 1960s and 1970s. Remember *Bewitched?* Recall Samantha's husband Darrin Stephens' role at ad agency McMann and Tate.

Each day, things burbled along predictably at McMann and Tate. Larry Tate, the bombastic cofounder of the agency, barked orders at Darrin, his senior account director. Dressed in his dark grey suit, Darrin arrived at the office knowing pretty much how his day would unfold. Even though the campaigns and clients changed, each day resembled the previous one. Darrin knew everyone in the agency, and everyone knew their roles. People stayed with the company—and in their same jobs—for years.

Despite all the client mishaps caused by mischievous or flawed spells cast by his wife's witchy relatives, Darrin kept his job and knew he would stay at McMann and Tate until he retired.

It's hard to believe that just over 40 years have passed since *Bewitched* premiered. The work scene depicted in the show seems almost unimaginable today. And recent TV programs make the contrast even sharper. To see what we mean, contrast Darrin Stephens with the cast of characters in *The Apprentice*.

"You're fired!" If you're an *Apprentice* devotee, you hear this phrase every week. Fortunately, it's coming from the boardroom at Trump Towers, and it's directed at someone other than you. But every week, like clockwork, someone leaves the show—and not happily. *The Apprentice* reflects the new world of work, where you're only as good as your last project. You can outperform everyone around you one week, but there's no guarantee that you won't get ousted the next. When your manager and the projects are changing all the time, as with *The Apprentice*, the successful strategy is not to conform but to continually distinguish yourself.

In today's workplace, creativity has trumped loyalty; individuality has replaced conformity; pro-activity has replaced hierarchy. You don't wait for job assignments—you create them. Those who succeeded on *The Apprentice* were aware of their talents and confident enough to use them to stand out and consistently deliver value to their teams.

With intense competition and pressure from shareholders to deliver ever-higher returns, companies have begun scrutinizing each employee to assess his or her value to the organization. If members of the executive team don't know you're there, then they figure they won't miss you when you're gone. Those who fly under the radar in corporations are the ones who hear "You're fired" for real. Today, this happens even to people who have served in the same organization for decades. When the inevitable need to reduce headcount arises, those who are not perceived as making unique and significant contributions are the first to be let go, often regardless of their tenure. The following story offers just one example.

MARGARET, SENIOR RN

Margaret worked at the same major metropolitan hospital for almost 30 years. During that time, she jumped through the myriad hoops the hospital began to demand, including getting a master's degree at age 60 simply to keep her job. Margaret did her job, and did it extremely well.

Yet, despite her advanced degree, extensive experience, and high praise from colleagues, Margaret was laid off via a letter delivered by FedEx after almost 30 years of loyal, excellent service to the hospital.

Increasingly many workers are suffering this experience, whether they worked for their company for 5 or 25 years.

In corporate positions, sales, independent business, and even politics and the media, people have realized that you need to "make a name for yourself" if you hope to stay in your profession. Those who can simply *do* the job won't receive nearly as many opportunities as those who carve out a unique niche for themselves. And the higher you move up the corporate ladder, the more important this personal branding becomes. It's all about adding value beyond what your colleagues deliver. It's about standing out, and standing for something special. Seth Godin put it this way in his blog:

> Most people, apparently, believe that if they just get their needle sharp enough, it'll magnetically leap out of the haystack and land wherever it belongs. If they don't get a great job or make a great sale or land a terrific date, it might just be because they don't deserve it. Having met some successful people, I can assure you that they didn't get that way by deserving it.
>
> What chance is there that your totally average resume, describing a totally average academic and work career is going to get you most jobs? "Hey Bill! Check out this average guy with an average academic background and really exceptionally average work experience! Maybe he's cheap!!"
>
> Do you hire people that way? Do you choose products that way? If you're driving a Chevy Cavalier and working for the Social Security Administration, perhaps, but those days are long gone.
>
> People are buying only one thing from you: the way the engagement (hiring you, working with you, dating you, using your product or service, learning from you) makes them feel.
>
> So how do you make people feel?
>
> Could you make them feel better? More? Could you create the emotions that they're seeking?
>
> As long as we focus on the commodity, on the sharper needle, we're lost. Why? Because most customers don't carry a magnet. Because the sharpest needle is rarely the one that gets out of the haystack. Instead, buyers are looking for the Free Prize, for that exceptional attribute that's worth talking about. I just polled the four interns sitting here with me. Between them, they speak 12 languages. No, that's not why I hired them. No, we don't need

Tagalog in our daily work . . . but it's a free prize. It's one of the many things that made them interesting, that made me feel good about hiring them.

Think about how *you* look for unique value in the products and services you purchase. For example, let's say you just received a speeding ticket. Depending on where you live, you can probably take a defensive-driving course to remove the ticket from your permanent record. In this case, it's not a matter of *whether* you take the course, but *where* you take it. Given the choice between a standard defensive-driving class and one that teaches with humor, or one created solely for "singles," which course are you more likely to choose? Most people will choose something other than the standard class. Why? Those courses offer *more* than just the basic requirements. They provide added value, and that makes them more intriguing and useful to you, the consumer.

The media and entertainment fields present additional examples. Actors often have a certain character type for which they have become known. Musicians and other artists build their image around personal attributes as well as their talent. Comedians find their "bit." Take Jack Nicholson. If you're like most people, his devilish eyebrows and borderline insane characters immediately come to mind. Think of Dennis Miller, and you instantly recall his classic sardonic, intellectual "rants."

To succeed in any professional endeavor, you must make your unique value *memorable*. No one should need to ask you what you bring to your position that's different or special. Your work, behavior, and demeanor should make this crystal clear to everyone around you.

In addition, when people understand how your skills and unique personal attributes support a larger goal that they care about, they remember you more readily. For example, perhaps you have a great sense of humor. Rather than just presenting yourself as the office clown, you might make yourself memorable by communicating why you use humor: "I find that laughter helps people relax and builds cooperation. I believe in leading through positive motivation." By making the link between your special ability with humor and an important business goal, you transform your attribute into an asset. And you send the unmistakable message that you stand for something important.

> *Insist on yourself; never imitate. . . . Every great man is unique.*
>
> —Ralph Waldo Emerson, American poet

Principle 2   Be Your Own Boss

To take the helm of your career and steer it toward your future, you must be your own boss—controlling your destiny, finding and seizing opportunities, and marching up the ramp of advancement in your profession. As your own boss, you decide which positions you will take, how much effort you'll invest in each job, and how you'll handle the challenges you'll inevitably encounter. You control how you present yourself and your intellectual and emotional assets, and even whom you position as your allies and your opponents.

At first blush, you might disagree. Perhaps you think your manager—or the CEO or board of directors—controls your future. Maybe you assume that your company's success—in the form of rising stock price, customer satisfaction, and profitability—will carry you indefinitely. We urge you *not* to count on outside forces to ensure your success. You can't control these forces—so you'll constantly be vulnerable to them. But you *do* control your own personal brand. Consider: Your skills and unique personal attributes don't disappear if your company's stock price plummets. Your future doesn't unravel if an executive who powerfully supported your advancement leaves the company. Your personal assets are yours, and no one can take them away from you. *You* must take responsibility for these assets, and use them to your advantage. In short, seek strength in yourself, not your circumstances.

Let's look at an example of someone who has thoroughly embraced the notion of being his own boss:

GARRY, SALES EXECUTIVE, PUBLISHING

Garry exudes confidence. He has worked as a sales executive in the same profession—publishing—for almost his entire career, but not the same company. Pricing in this industry used to be highly subjective, allowing for great profits. Now, with stiffer competition, most companies in the industry are struggling to cut costs so they can offer lower prices. But still Garry is on top.

Why? Even though he works for a corporation, he has never tied his identity to a company. He could switch employers tomorrow, and the change wouldn't cause more than a brief ripple in his monthly sales. His customers buy from him because of who he is and what he does for them, not the product he sells.

How has he created this loyalty? Garry's personal brand has the following qualities:

- He builds relationships with customers and connects them with each other.

- He provides an enjoyable experience to his clients by shielding them from messy details and ensuring that they are known to those throughout the organization.

Garry knows his greatest assets and consistently displays these in everything he does.

Principle 3   Forget the Ladder: It's a Ramp

Many people still think of their career as a ladder with their ultimate goal being that top rung. Even from the bottom, you can see the top rung off in the distance. You climb the ladder, progressing in your career one milestone at a time. At each rung, you work hard on what you are doing at the moment. You forget about that next step because you're sure you'll get there when the right time comes without encountering any obstacles. You fall into complacency.

Then something happens.

Perhaps you make it happen:

- You realize one day that you feel bored and unchallenged.
- You begin craving more responsibility.
- You decide that you want more pay.
- You feel an urge to try something new.
- You realize that you've had your fill of a nasty boss or an uncomfortable organizational culture.

Perhaps the something comes from outside your control:

- Your company decides it's time to "right-size."
- The product you're working on gets canceled.
- The industry you work in is hit by a destructive scandal.
- Your manager leaves the company, taking several team members with her, and the company decides to eliminate your job.

Only when that something happens do you think about that next rung in your career ladder. You put together your resume, reconnect with lost professional contacts, and so forth. You expend enormous effort connecting with recruiters, writing cover letters, refining your career marketing materials, searching through job boards—all the fallback methods that people used back when the world of work was predictable.

But in today's knowledge economy, this sporadic, effortful approach to career management isn't the best approach. Instead, you have to get rid of the ladder metaphor and view your career climb as a ramp. When you're ascending a ramp, you don't stop and relax—you're constantly advancing in perpetual motion toward your professional goals. In this scenario, you don't wait for a trigger to move you to your next step in your career: You manage that movement yourself, every day of your life:

- You update and revise your resume in real time.
- You maintain networking contacts, rather than letting them fade away.
- You seek out tasks and activities that will move you closer to your goals.
- You apply your strengths and unique talents to every task you undertake.

Perhaps you're thinking, "This sounds like a lot more work than climbing a ladder." But in fact, perpetual career management is a lot *less* work. That's because you build momentum: Once you adopt this mindset and make the corresponding behaviors part of your regular routine, you never have to make a focused effort to work on your career again. Instead, you're always thinking about it and tweaking it as a matter of course. It's like brushing your teeth in the morning: Career management becomes something you just do.

Let's be clear that we are talking about a ramp, not an escalator. On a ramp, you are still in control. You're ascending the ramp by moving your own feet forward. You are responsible for reaching the top. You are mindful of the actions necessary to propel yourself forward. On an escalator, you're standing there helplessly, as the mechanism moves you up. You are giving away control and hoping to arrive at (rather than working toward) your desired destination.

Principle 4   Think Like a Brand

If these elements of the *Career Distinction* mindset sound familiar, that's not surprising. Corporate marketers have used them for years.

It's called *branding*. But the *Career Distinction* mindset puts you in position to brand *yourself*, not a company or product.

And while corporate branding typically requires scores of ad execs and million-dollar marketing budgets, personal branding requires only you. You are your own 24/7 billboard and interactive ad campaign. Every day, in everything you do, you tell the world about yourself, your values, your goals, and your skills. In fact, you already have a brand—even if you don't know what it is, and even if it isn't working for you the way you'd like it to.

The 1-2-3 Success! process presented in this book helps you clarify the personal brand you need to create in order to achieve career distinction—and then communicate that brand unerringly to those around you. In the next chapter, you'll gain a clearer understanding of branding (including common myths about it) as well as learn more about personal branding's origins and the nature of the personal-branding process.

> *Everyone has a chance to be a brand worthy of remark.*
>
> —Tom Peters, management guru

Chapter 3

Brand Yourself for Career Success

In this chapter, you will learn:

- What personal branding really is—including common myths about it
- The power of personal branding
- The steps in the 1-2-3 Success! personal branding process

Personal branding enables you to profit from what distinguishes you from others with similar skills and abilities. Made popular by management guru Tom Peters in his 1997 *Fast Company* article "The Brand Called You," personal branding is not a fad. And it's not just for CEOs. In the decade since personal branding emerged, thousands of companies and independent consultants have begun offering personal branding services to career-minded professionals in virtually every country around the globe. Indeed, ExecuNet called personal branding the number one tool for executive job seekers.

In the six years since the founding of Reach, we have certified more than 150 career coaches, human resources executives, image consultants, and resume writers to deliver to their clients the Reach Personal Branding methodology that we present in this book. Moreover, we have helped tens of thousands of professionals build their personal brands through our workshops, newsletters, e-learning programs, and teleseminars. Personal branding is so powerful that Fortune 500 companies—firms single-mindedly focused on their *corporate* brands—are helping employees build their *personal* brands. Companies like JPMorgan, IBM, Microsoft, Disney, British Telecom, Warner Bros., and American Express have incorporated Reach's personal branding workshops into their professional development programs.

Simply put, personal branding has gone mainstream. It's the most effective and innovative strategy you can use to achieve professional success *and* fulfillment. Once a luxury, now a necessity, personal branding is the constant in today's rapidly changing world of work.

But before we go into greater detail about personal branding, let's talk a little about branding in general—especially the many misconceptions about what it is and why it's valuable. We're sure you'll appreciate the true power of branding once you replace myths with truths.

Myth 1: Branding is just for giant corporations and products on the grocery store shelf.

Truth: Branding isn't just for corporations and products. Look around you. The Red Cross, New York City, Silicon Valley—they're all brands. So are Richard Branson, Tom Ford, and Oprah. In fact, Oprah showed up in the top-10 North American brands in Brandchannel's Reader's Choice Awards—between Coke and Amazon.com. The lesson? Everything, every place, every organization (whether it offers products or services), and every person can be a brand. And yes, that means you!

Myth 2: Branding is the latest fad.

Truth: Branding wasn't invented by the Nikes or Coca-Cola companies of this world. Since before industrial times, people have used branding to develop strong, enduring relationships with customers. Medieval townspeople and villagers who frequented Mr. Alain's pie shop knew that his pies tasted especially good and were always handed out with a warm smile. Mr. Alain made customers feel so special that they didn't mind taking the long walk, waiting in line, and paying the extra two pence the pies cost. Today, branding still provides those same benefits—though on a larger, more global scale.

Myth 3: A brand is a logo or tag line.

Truth: According to whatis.com, a brand is "a product, service, or concept that is publicly distinguished from other products, services, or concepts so that it can be easily communicated and usually marketed." A brand is a company's most valuable asset. Branding is *not* just a logo or tag line. And it's not just a bunch of marketing activities (advertising, direct mail, and so forth). It's the sum of an organization's or person's actions, communications, offerings, and interactions.

> *The brand is the amusement park. The product is the souvenir.*
>
> —Nick Graham, chief underpants officer, Joe Boxer

Myth 4: Branding is about creating an image.

Truth: Consumers today are too sophisticated to be fooled by mere images of the unique value a company has to offer. Successful brands don't just create images: They *deliver* on their unique promise of value. For example, Volvo differentiates itself from other car makers by its promise of safety and security. If Volvos began exploding on impact during collisions, consumers would no longer connect Volvo with safety—regardless of the number of ads they saw in which actors claimed that their Volvo was so safe it "saved my life." Similarly, people would not associate Disney with wholesome family entertainment if the company decided to open a chain of gambling casinos and adult entertainment centers. Just as Milli Vanilli disappeared once their fans learned they were lip-synching, brands can survive only by consistently delivering on their unique value. Branding is not about creating an artificial image of unique value for the outside world. It's about *actually* providing that unique value.

> *A brand for a company is like a reputation for a person.*
> *You earn reputation by trying to do hard things well.*
>   —Jeff Bezos, founder and CEO of Amazon.com

Myth 5: Branding requires big bucks.

Truth: It doesn't take multimillion dollar ad campaigns to build strong brands. Just look at Starbucks. It is one of the world's strongest brands, and it is never advertised on television. Branding is more of a philosophy than it is a marketing expense item. Done right, branding is part of the DNA of a company or a person. It is built through every activity, every interaction, every decision. Successful branding requires commitment and consistency not cash.

Corporations benefit from strong branding in many ways. Branding enables them to:

- *Charge a premium for their products and services.* Ever think about why you're paying so much for a Starbucks coffee, when the coffee shop next door charges about half the price?
- *Increase their market valuation.* Only 10 percent of Coca-Cola's market valuation derives from the company's physical assets.

The strength of its brand accounts for almost 90 percent of that valuation. Coke is currently the world's strongest brand, according to an Interbrand study.[1]

- *Extend their product or service lines.* Marriott has used its strong brand name to create new chains of hotels (such as Marriott Courtyard) for a different target market (in this case, business travelers who wanted a more homelike experience, or families traveling with children). If Volvo wanted to get into the home-security business, it could probably do so relatively effortlessly by bringing its brand value into its new endeavor.

- *Thrive during an economic downturn.* Strong brands survive difficult times. Consider who survived the dot-com bust. It was the strong technology brands with enduring customer relationships—such as IBM and Apple. The smaller, younger dot-coms who expected to prevail have virtually disappeared.

- *Attract and retain quality employees and partners.* Do you know anyone who would rather work for a struggling, unknown company than for a strong brand? We all want our resumes to boast lengthy experience with strong brand names. When we associate ourselves with these brands, our own professional reputations shine.

Branding is valuable to companies because it helps consumers distinguish among seemingly similar offerings. Do you drink Coca-Cola or Pepsi? Do you shop at Target or Wal-Mart? Do you get your coffee at Starbucks or Dunkin Donuts on the way to work in the morning? Would you rather live in Los Angeles or New York? Do you fly Virgin Upper Class or British Airways Club World?

People also feel strongly attached to the brands they've chosen. Some Pepsi drinkers wouldn't even consider drinking another cola. And try getting an Apple evangelist to touch the keyboard of a PC. The next time you are in the grocery store, note how you almost automatically reach for certain brands despite the huge number of alternative products that are available. Ask yourself why you made that brand choice.

In fact, people's *consumer* brand choices provide clues about their own *personal* brands. Think about it: What do your car, home, watch, wardrobe, eyeglasses, favorite restaurant—every brand you've chosen—say about *you*?

Personal branding is vital to advancing your career. After all, there are many other people out there who share your desired job title. If you work in an organization, you want your boss, hiring managers, and executive recruiters to choose *you*. And if you're running your own business, you want your customers to choose *you*. Even more, you want them to seek you out.

That's where personal branding comes in.

The 1-2-3 Success! Personal Branding Process

Personal branding is the most effective way to clarify and communicate what makes you different, special, and valuable to employers and customers—and use those qualities to guide your career. It's about unearthing your unique attributes—your strengths, skills, values, and passions—and using them to stand out from your peers or competitors. Thus, through personal branding, you clearly communicate the *unique promise of value* that you have to offer. Think of your personal brand as your reputation. It builds over time and becomes synonymous with how people describe you.

Over the past six years, tens of thousands of professionals, executives, and entrepreneurs have undertaken the powerful process of self-understanding, positioning, and communication described in the remaining chapters of this book. They have emerged from this process with a clearer understanding of who they are and how they can expand their success through the consistent expression of their personal brands. The process they've followed consists of three steps: Extract, Express, and Exude. (See Figure 3.1.)

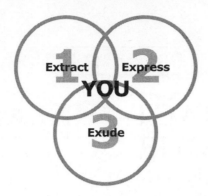

Figure 3.1   The 1-2-3 Success! Process

In the chapters that follow, we give you the tools you need to begin behaving as a brand. And we help you adopt the *Career Distinction* mindset necessary to benefit from this potent technique. In the Extract phase, you embark on a mission of self-discovery, whereby you describe the unique and valuable brand called *you*. In the Express Phase, you build a plan to increase your visibility and credibility among those who will help you reach your career goals. And in the Exude phase, you ensure that everything about you and everything that surrounds you sends a consistent, on-brand message about who you are and what you bring to the table.

As we've noted, your personal brand is the one constant in today's ever-changing world of work. Like a trusty beacon, it guides you to your destination: a satisfying, successful career.

Turn to Chapter 4 now to discover how to begin unearthing your unique promise of value.

Note

1. "The 100 Top Brands 2006," *BusinessWeek Online*, http://bwnt .businessweek.com/brand/2006.

EXTRACT—UNEARTH YOUR UNIQUE PROMISE OF VALUE

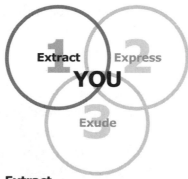

Extract
- Know Yourself to Grow Yourself
- Remember, It's What They Think That Counts
- Define Your Brand Community
- Tell Your Brand Story

The Extract phase of the personal branding process lays the foundation for the rest of the process. It helps you uncover and understand everything about your personal brand and how your brand fits into the bigger picture. In the following four chapters, you will discover how to gather insights about your personal brand based on your own self-assessment and information from others. You'll also identify your brand community and learn how to tell a compelling story that communicates your brand.

Chapter 4

Know Yourself
to Grow Yourself

In this chapter, you will learn:

- How to unearth your unique promise of value
- What your vision, purpose, goals, values, and passions are

Your personal brand is your unique promise of value. It's what those around you expect from you—what you're known for. Just as Volvo is known for safety and Apple is known for "thinking different," your personal brand ensures that you're recognized and appreciated for the relevant and compelling value you provide. We have all heard the expression "your reputation precedes you." Having a reputation is powerful. It becomes your calling card, trumpeting your unique promise of value long before you talk with your boss about your next role at the company; meet with a job interviewer at a new firm; or network with potential customers, investors, and partners for a new enterprise you're considering launching.

To build a solid reputation that will catapult you toward your goals, you must understand and be able to articulate what makes you exceptional and compelling. Each of us is unique. We have our own individual combination of talents, skills, and interests that enable us to fulfill our ultimate purpose in life. This chapter helps you uncover your unique promise of value. This extraction process takes time, effort, and some patience. It requires you to think hard about who you are and what makes you unique. Even for those who are very self-aware and introspective, this step can require a significant investment. The primary objective of the Extract phase is to define your:

- Vision
- Purpose
- Goals
- Values
- Passions

The process for defining these things resembles that used by organizations. When corporations set out to cultivate their brands, they conduct internal and external research and then analyze their findings to articulate their brand from the perspective of their customers and employees. You will be doing your own self-exploration and analysis to understand *your* brand—drawing on your own insights as well as seeking input from those who know you. Your own assessment gives you only part of the picture of your brand. Obtaining candid input from others helps you fill in the rest of the picture. This chapter focuses on your internal assessment of your unique promise of value, while Chapter 5 turns to your external sources of information.

As you work through this chapter, you'll find references to exercises that you can explore in our companion workbook, which you can download by visiting www.careerdistinction.com/workbook. Because these exercises encourage you to dig deeply into some personal themes, some of them might seem a little "touchy-feely." We urge you to keep an open mind and to complete the exercises over a period of time (or repeat them a few times) to get comfortable with the material. This is not a linear process. If you feel stuck while completing one exercise, move on to another.

The exercises in our companion workbook represent just a small sample of the many additional activities available in our branding toolboxes. Those presented in the workbook have proved the most useful to our executive clients. If you have recently taken some quantitative career assessments through a career coach or know of other exercises or activities that work for you, by all means, incorporate these as well.

Articulating Your Vision and Purpose

Before you can clearly describe your personal brand, you need to look at the bigger picture: your vision and purpose. Your vision is *external*. It's what you see as possible for the world. Your purpose is *internal*. It's the role you might play in helping the world to realize that vision.

Many people find understanding and documenting their vision and purpose the most challenging part of the Extract phase. That isn't surprising: Few of us walk around routinely thinking about our vision for the world and our role in supporting that vision. We're typically much more wrapped up in mundane, day-to-day matters. We spend our time fighting the fires of the day, working to complete as many of our "to-do" tasks as possible, and preparing for tomorrow's meetings. So don't be discouraged if this part takes some time.

> *We go where our vision is.*
>
> —Joseph Murphy, author of
> *The Power of Your Subconscious Mind*

Before working on these exercises for yourself, consider the following example of an executive who has achieved tremendous success by knowing his vision and living his purpose.

CHRISTOPHE GINISTY, MANAGING DIRECTOR, RUMEUR PUBLIQUE

Christophe Ginisty leads a one-of-a-kind communications firm that is sure about what it is and what it is not. He focuses his communications company's strategy on his vision: *a world where everyone, regardless of income or geography, has access to the benefits of technology.* His *purpose* (his role in supporting that vision) is *to be a leader in a major social revolution that will bring the benefits of technology to those in need.* Today, Rumeur Publique is a leading information technology (IT) communications firm in Europe. Among its target market (IT businesses), the company is recognized as a cutting-edge firm that provides superior service. In fact, Ginisty's brand can boast a large percentage of the world's strongest IT brands as clients.

But about a year into his venture, Ginisty's lawyer and accountant suggested that his vision was too narrow and was limiting his revenue opportunities. Concerned about his ability to bring in enough revenue to sustain his business, they recommended either closing down the business or widening its scope. But Ginisty remained faithful to his vision and purpose. He turned away business that was not relevant to his brand, such as opportunities to manage public relations for cosmetics and fashion houses in Paris. As you can imagine, turning away business is hard to do when you're starting up a new enterprise and struggling to meet payroll demands. But Ginisty's commitment to his vision and purpose paid off.

He remains dedicated to his original vision and continues to focus on spreading the word about the benefits of technology. He's also expanding his business and is starting new ventures linked to his vision and the Rumeur Publique brand. For example, he's considering opening a restaurant where IT executives can meet, talk, and move the whole industry forward. He has also laid plans for a speakers' bureau that will continue to get the message out about the benefits of technology. In addition, he has started a foundation that will bring the benefits of technology to areas of the world that need it.

Finally, he is creating a festival that will be for the Internet what the Cannes Festival is to movies. This festival will honor and award people who have used the Internet to get their creative work noticed. There will be categories such as Best Video, Best Photography, and Best Citizen Journalism acknowledging talented people who have leveraged technology to achieve their goals. This new effort strongly supports Ginisty's vision of bringing the benefits of technology to those who need it. Festival winners won't be technologists, but people who have benefited from the use of technology to get their work distributed, seen, and critiqued.

To articulate your vision and purpose, visit www.careerdistinction .com/workbook now.

Clarifying Your Goals

It's great to understand your vision and purpose. But you can't fulfill your purpose without also clarifying your goals. Your goals help direct the actions you need to carry out in order to fulfill your purpose. This direction is vital: As the great Yogi Berra once said, "If you don't know where you're going, you'll end up some place else."

Goals thus enable you to chart a course to your destination—fulfilling your purpose and vision. For example, if your vision is a pollution-free world and your purpose is to get others to understand their personal impact on the environment, your goals might include:

- Starting a recycling program at work.
- Forming an environmental group.

- Becoming a noted speaker on the topic of personal environmental responsibility.
- Training in carbon emissions.
- Writing a business plan for an environmental consulting business.

In addition to providing direction, goals encourage you to focus. By keeping your goals top-of-mind, you allocate your time and energy to the courses of action that support achievement of your purpose and vision—rather than squandering these precious resources on less relevant activities.

> *In the absence of clearly defined goals, we become strangely loyal to performing daily trivia until ultimately we become enslaved by it.*
> —Robert Heinlein, author of science fiction

Last, goals help you stretch yourself. They make you reach a little bit further than you might otherwise strive. Sadly, most people spend more time planning their vacations each year than thinking about what they want to do with their lives. The trick to clarifying your goals is to set them high. A goal needs to be something that you have to stretch to attain. For example, last year, William delivered 38 speaking events. If he were to say, "I'm going to do 40 speaking events this year," that wouldn't be a stretch for him. But if he said, "I'm going to do 60 speaking events," then he's extending much further. He may only get to 52; but he's going to land many more than if he had set his goal at 40.

Of course, some people have always known their major goal. At four years old, they knew they wanted to grow up and be a plastic surgeon, a firefighter, or a teacher. And since that time, they've steadfastly pursued this aspiration. Madonna, an incredibly strong brand herself, is one of those people. She said from a very early age, I'm going to be either a famous singer and dancer or a nun.

Though some people do know their goals very early in life, most of us have to think about the various possibilities, consider different scenarios, and gain experience in different kinds of work before being able to clarify our goals and see how they support our vision and purpose. Visit www.careerdistinction.com/workbook to explore an exercise that helps you define your goals.

Tip: Write down or print out your goals and post them where you will see them every day, like on the bathroom mirror or right above your office phone.

Identifying Your Values and Passions

There is no greater source of peace and fulfillment than living the life you want to live. Yet, most of us find ourselves well into our adult lives when we suddenly wonder whether we've "missed the boat." We ask ourselves, "There has to be something more, right?"

There *is* something more—and you can make it happen by identifying your values and passions. Your values are your operating principles and part of your belief system. You take them with you wherever you go. For example, Kirsten's values include intelligence, independence, pro-activity, family, flexibility, and making a difference. Knowing your values is crucial for making career decisions, because it helps you recognize whether you and a particular organization would make a good match. For instance, if you value family, you would be far more productive in and satisfied with your work in an organization that is highly ranked in the *Working Mother's* list of 100 Best Companies. The story that follows reveals the importance of living your values through your work.

KRIS APPEL, BUDDING SOCIAL ENTREPRENEUR

Kris worked for a well-known government agency for nearly 20 years—until boredom kicked in and she moved to a technology company in the private sector. Although not an easy task in a government agency, Kris had moved quickly into the executive ranks, thriving on innovation, making processes better, and delivering impressive results. She was the person her colleagues called on to get any mission-critical project done, in any part of the organization. She felt highly energized by her work.

Then the technology company was sold. The management team offered a buyout or relocation to the new headquarters in India. Kris chose the buyout, expecting that she would easily find a new position. She worked with Deb Dib, known as the CEO Coach, on her branding and they discovered that Kris was an intrapreneur—a person who demonstrates an entrepreneurial spirit within an organization. As an intrapreneur, she valued—and needed—freedom to create change, to make things happen.

Kris received several good offers during her job search, but she found it difficult to replicate the culture that had previously allowed her the intrapreneurial freedom and breadth of responsibility she craved. She was disheartened, but refused to settle for less.

As often happens for people who attend to their personal brand, the disappointment proved short-lived: A new opportunity emerged—one that was ideal for her brand. The opportunity? A highly selective university program designed to help women executives create viable new businesses in technology.

Since joining the program, Kris has sharpened her focus on intrapreneurship. She has partnered with two women to start a company to manufacture a pioneering device that will be instrumental in restoring quality of life to certain medical patients. She has also decided to end her job search, build the new company, and do philanthropic work in her community. By being true to her personal brand, Kris is now living her dream.

Tip: To better understand your values, take
note when something occurs that bothers you and
ask yourself why it makes you upset. Chances are
one of your values is being violated.

But identifying your values isn't enough. You also need to articulate your passions—the activities that most energize you. For example, Richard Branson, the British entrepreneur best known for his Virgin brand, has a consuming passion for adventure. Martha Stewart's overriding passion is for entertaining. And Bill Gates has a passion for technology.

In addition to fueling better on-the-job performance, your passions also make you memorable. Many people have discovered that talking about their passions during development discussions with their boss or during job interviews makes them more energized and interesting to hiring managers—even if their passions are not directly related to the position at hand.

And even if your colleagues don't share your passions, they will likely respect and admire you for having them. One of William's clients expresses her passion for all things humorous with the joke of the week she posts on her door, the true-life funny stories she uses to start all of her meetings, and her top-10 list of the world's funniest people. Another client who is passionate about health has started an after-work yoga class, designed a health-food menu for the company cafeteria, and provides daily health tips at the bottom of his internal e-mail messages.

DAVE, SOFTWARE SALES LEADER EXTRAORDINAIRE

Dave leads a team of sales directors who sell infrastructure software to IT executives. Dave's passion is team sports—of all types. He knows every statistic, every player, every ballpark. He visits every sporting-goods store, plays football or baseball every weekend with friends, and watches ESPN as if it were the only channel on TV.

Earlier in his life, Dave struggled to see how he might connect his love of sports to his work in IT software sales. He thought he had two options: keep his passions and his work separate *or* quit his job in IT software and find work selling tickets for his local ball club.

Having grown accustomed to the finer things in life, he decided to keep his day job and focus on sports in his free time.

William challenged Dave to think about how he might make a connection between what he does and what he's passionate about. Finally, he said, "I've figured it out. It was right there in front of me all the time." Since most of his team's clients are at least mildly interested in sports, he decided he would use sports metaphors in his sales presentations. To involve his whole team, he initiated a contest. (One of Dave's values is competition.) The salesperson who designed the best new presentation with a sports theme would receive a special bonus. This contest reinvigorated his team—and generated spectacular results. Sales increased, Dave's team felt more engaged in their work, and Dave himself felt more fulfilled by his career. Not only did he enjoy the competitive spirit he had unleashed in his team; he was also thrilled with the new level of energy and commitment he saw in his salesforce.

As Dave's story reveals, there are always creative ways to connect your passions to what you do and how you do it. And, often it's this creative combination that differentiates your brand. For example, when Kirsten realized that she could successfully marry her passion for technology with her passion for helping people gain control of their own career success, her brand came into sharp focus.

Sadly, many people are disconnected from their passions. If you have this difficulty, go to www.careerdistinction.com/workbook to find a helpful exercise for identifying the activities that most energize you.

> My passions were all gathered together like fingers that made a fist. Drive is considered aggression today; I knew it then as purpose.
>
> —Bette Davis, Academy Award winning actress

Chapter 5

Remember, It's What They Think That Counts

In this chapter, you will learn:

- How to get external feedback on your brand
- What brand attributes are
- Why it's important to leverage your strengths

In Chapter 4, you identified your vision, purpose, goals, values, and passions in order to begin articulating the unique contribution you want to make to the world through your personal brand. But as with any brand, your personal brand ultimately exists in *other* people's hearts and minds. So in addition to knowing key aspects of yourself, you must also attune yourself to external perceptions of you.

If you're an executive, you probably have limited information about what others really think of you. The higher you move in the company, the more you hear what people think you *want* to hear. And the less you hear what you need to know. Sometimes even one clear insight from an outside observer—"You need to delegate more," "You intimidate people"—can forever change the course of your career. Savvy executives don't wait for that insight; they proactively seek out the honest feedback they need to be ever more effective as they progress through their careers.

> CEO *reputations have a significant impact on a company's success and viability. CEO reputation, when harnessed on behalf of corporate goals, is an asset.*
> —Leslie Gaines-Ross, author of *CEO Capital*

One of William's clients, the president of a software company, was truly confident about what those around him thought of him. That was, of course, until he asked them. When he received personal brand feedback from his employees, colleagues, and customers, he developed a whole new picture of his external reputation. Externally, his self-confidence was being perceived as arrogance; his speed and dynamism were making him seem dismissive; and his pensive nature was being interpreted as disinterest. William really earned his consulting fee when he had to share these delicate insights with his client; but to his client's credit, not only did he graciously receive this feedback, he proactively developed a plan to refine his reputation to align it more with his own brand understanding.

As you may have concluded while reading Chapter 4, a successful personal brand is authentic: It reflects your unique *personal* attributes or qualities. That's why you need to know yourself before you can build a successful brand. If you're creative, dynamic, outgoing, and whimsical, you'll find it difficult to succeed by communicating personal-brand attributes of predictable, steady, and focused. When it comes to understanding your brand attributes, you need input from those who know you.

What Are Brand Attributes?

What are brand attributes, exactly? They are the adjectives people use to describe you. We all walk around citing people's brand attributes without even realizing it. "Have you met Sally? She's the most dedicated assistant we have in this company." Or, "I'd like to introduce you to Henry, he is so buttoned up that he can tell you where every dollar of the budget is being spent."

Your goal is to understand the attributes that people associate with *you*. That way, you can maximize the most attractive and compelling ones—those that will help you stand out from everyone around you.

Tip: When people introduce you to others, listen to what they are communicating about your brand attributes.

Each of us possesses a unique combination of rational and emotional brand attributes. Typically, *rational* brand attributes relate to your competencies. They are the "table stakes" that get you into the game. For example, if you are a competent accounting manager, your rational brand attributes would include your ability to understand financial statements. Organizations have rational brand attributes, too. For an automobile manufacturer, for example, reliability is a rational brand attribute. Consumers won't even consider buying a car that is unreliable. But reliability alone won't make a person choose one car over another. It's the emotional brand attributes that tip the scales. *Emotional* attributes (such as "luxurious" or "sexy" or "safe") are the ones that forge strong connections between people and their preferred brands.

Many years ago, when William was working at IBM, the company participated in a study that sought to determine the ideal brand attributes that would tip the scales in favor of one middleware vendor over another. They were surprised at the results. Traditionally conservative IT Business to Business decision makers consistently identified what turned out to be emotional brand attributes as determining factors. Sure, the products need to be reliable and secure. Those rational brand attributes ensure that a vendor is considered in the first place. But among those vendors who met the rational criteria, the emotional connections proved pivotal.

These findings probably shouldn't have come as a surprise. After all, we *are* human. And even the most rational person (whether he admits it or not) is influenced by emotion. In his book *LoveMarks* (Powerhouse Books, Brooklyn, NY, 2005), Saatchi and Saatchi CEO, Kevin Roberts argues even more strongly for the connection between emotion and the success of certain brands. He illustrates how some brands just command greater loyalty, thanks to their powerful emotional attributes. He calls these brands LoveMarks and maintains that they inspire loyalty beyond reason.

> **Love:** v. A *deep, tender, ineffable feeling of affection* and solicitude toward a person, such as that arising from kinship, *recognition of attractive qualities*, or a sense of underlying oneness.

All You Need Is Love: The Power of Emotional Brand Attributes

All this talk about emotions and successful brands is music to the ears of anyone who wants to get ahead by leveraging his or her personal brand—whether that means advancing in his or her current organization or moving to another employer or business opportunity. If emotional brand attributes are so critical to loyalty, then who better to win loyalty from the people around you than *you*—a human being? You certainly have an edge over products and companies.

But don't get us wrong. Being loved is not about pleasing everyone. As an executive, you inevitably must make decisions that are unpopular with some people. Strong brands take a stand; they don't try to be all things to all people. But developing emotional connections with your constituencies will ensure that people respect you even if they don't agree with everything you do. You build these connections by consistently demonstrating your emotional brand attributes. Also, you need to augment your emotional brand attributes with a sturdy foundation of rational brand attributes. As we've seen, those attributes illustrate your competence and make you credible. Even the most *lovable* among us won't get too far without being able to demonstrate that we're capable and generate business results. The most winning brands succeed by exuding a solid combination of genuine rational *and* emotional brand attributes—as the story that follows reveals.

LAUREN, ONCOLOGY NURSE

Lauren is an incredibly compassionate oncology nurse. She cares deeply about all her patients. Everyone in the close-knit field of oncology nursing knew of Lauren and her remarkable compassion.

True, many nurses are compassionate: This ability is part of their job and perhaps the trait that attracted them to the field. Thus, compassion is a rational brand attribute in this profession. But in Lauren, this attribute is off the charts. It's so strong in her that it has enabled her to build her professional reputation on it. Lauren also combines her compassion with her passion for medicine to help her patients manage their lives and reduce the stress and pain they're experiencing.

Lauren's reputation has enabled her to excel in her career. When a renowned West Coast hospital with a large oncology department was looking for a special nurse to be part of a cancer treatment program for terminally ill patients, Lauren was recruited. The program involved intensive, sometimes painful treatments. The physicians administering the treatments needed a nurse who was an expert in the field and who had a uniquely supportive and caring demeanor. They also needed someone who could help patients manage pain and remain optimistic in the face of physical challenges and discouraging odds.

The only way to help the patients make it through the program was to provide constant positive reinforcement and compassion—Lauren's brand. She has become the star of the program and has begun training other nurses in her technique of pain mediation. She continues to exude her brand attribute of compassion—standing out in a field where this attribute makes a vital difference.

Shining the Spotlight on Positive Brand Attributes

In addition to having rational and emotional brand attributes, we all have positive and negative brand attributes. For example, perhaps you are energetic, enthusiastic, and collaborative (your positive attributes), but also impatient and hasty (negative attributes). The goal in personal branding is to showcase your *positive* brand attributes while diminishing your *negative* ones. Remember, the exciting thing about branding is that it gives you permission to maximize your strengths and other attractive qualities.

> *Anyone can revolt. It is more difficult silently to obey our own inner promptings, and to spend our lives finding sincere and fitting means of expression for our temperament and our gifts.*
>
> —Georges Rouault, French artist

Entire companies strengthen their brand by applying these practices. Consider IBM, once known for being old fashioned and bureaucratic. The company implemented organizational changes so as to focus more on the future and create a less bureaucratic culture. At the same time, it launched a major e-business marketing campaign to communicate these positive changes to the world. The campaign paid big dividends: Now, most people see "Big Blue" as leading the Internet revolution rather than remaining mired in the slow-moving, giant mainframe computer environment.

How to Identify Your Own Brand Attributes?

This book comes with a 15-day password to a special *Career Distinction* version of 360°Reach, the leading personal branding assessment. You will be able to use this one-of-a-kind tool to help you understand how you are perceived by those around you. Once you've obtained feedback from 360°Reach, you can identify those attributes that will help you be *most* successful.

There is one password per purchased book. To learn about this assessment and the terms of use, please go to www.careerdistinction.com/360Reach.

But asking for feedback is not a one-time event. Perhaps your 360°Reach assessment will be the first time you have formally polled those around you; you must continue to ask for feedback. In fact, you must become a feedback fanatic. You must seek it out regularly.

Whether William is in New York or Kuala Lumpur, at the end of every workshop he delivers, he asks the participants to go to the flip charts at the front of the room and write down his top brand attribute. He keeps his back to the flipcharts so his participants can be completely candid. He has spent a full day, sometimes two or three days, with the participants—so he wants to understand their impressions of his brand. He saves all the flip chart pages so he can see if he is consistently demonstrating his most compelling brand attributes. For this book, he consolidated the input from all the flip charts. Here are his top five personal brand attributes:

1. Enthusiastic
2. Passionate
3. Energetic

4.   Confident

5.   International

A Note about Your Strengths

It's unfortunate that so many executive development programs concentrate on helping learners address their weaknesses instead of maximizing what they already have going for them—their most natural gifts and talents. In personal branding, it is essential to understand and use your strengths—your skills and capabilities. Of course, weaknesses deserve some acknowledgment and attention, but you should devote most of your energy to identifying and leveraging the skills that you enjoy *and* do well. We call these *motivated skills*. Why focus on using your motivated skills? Doing so enables you to derive the *most* satisfaction from your career while differentiating you from your peers. As you go about your days, you can identify these skills by paying attention to how you feel as your day progresses. What are you doing at your workplace when you feel the happiest? What skills would you relish employing even if you weren't paid to use them?

Many of us are good at a lot of things, but we don't enjoy using *all* our skills. For example, perhaps you excel at analyzing market research reports, but you absolutely loathe that kind of work. If you had to do this work all day every day, you'd soon be looking for a new job. For you, analyzing market research reports is a *burnout skill*. Be sure to identify your burnout skills and omit them from your brand communications. After all, if you list a burnout skill in your resume, you may unwittingly end up doing it again in your next job.

Tip: At the end of each day, remind yourself of how you used a strength to solve a problem or add value to your employer. This is empowering and reinforces your strengths so you will use them regularly.

Although introspection can help you identify your motivated skills, you should further validate them by examining your 360°Reach results. For example, you may have important strengths that others don't perceive, or you may not be aware of strengths that others clearly see in you. Let's look at an example of someone who truly understands his strengths.

TOM MONHEIM, PRICING LEADER

Tom uncovered his strengths of creative thinking and analytics and combines them to be uniquely valuable to marketing organizations. It is rare to find someone with these two disparate strengths, yet Tom's 360°Reach assessment clearly identifies these strengths.

Tom collaborates with teams to innovate pricing solutions that deliver substantial profit growth. With Fortune 500 leadership experience in marketing, finance, and IT, he is positioned to equip businesses with the ideal mix of strategy, analytics, and technology to unlock revenue potential through intelligent pricing. Success in this niche requires a distinctive blend of creative and logical thinking to address the art as well as science of strategic price management. The creative realm of pricing must go far beyond "the numbers," and into aspects such as exploring original ways to segment the business, appraising consumer value perceptions, and crafting innovative pricing structures and value bundles. Tom's creative traits have been honed through executive leadership positions in marketing, strategic planning, and of course, strategic pricing.

Tom's vision is to help organizations and individuals achieve remarkable functional and financial growth. As a pricing professional, he's committed to becoming a highly visible thought leader and speaker in the strategic pricing arena and a pioneer in developing innovative pricing solutions that optimize profit. Outside of his day job, Tom is involved in real estate investing and helping people improve their lives through better money management.

"The Strengths Movement" explained in the box that follows provides additional insights into the importance of leveraging your motivated skills. In addition, try the strengths exercise in the workbook (www.careerdistinction.com/workbook).

The Strengths Movement

The Gallup Organization has initiated an entire movement related to strengths-based management, which you can learn more about by reading *Now, Discover Your Strengths* by Marcus Buckingham and Donald O. Clifton. (The Free Press, New York, NY, 2001) The strengths movement is founded on the belief that people progress more rapidly in their careers when they use their greatest talents. But unfortunately, most of us are taught from a young age to focus on addressing our weaknesses rather than using our strengths. And it's not surprising. Despite the fact that you were doing third grade math, your first grade teacher ignored it and told you that your penmanship was not perfect and asked you to work on it. Your manager in your first job told you that you were great at communicating and presenting but that your project management skills were lacking, so she sent you to a project management workshop. We all have this mistaken belief that to be more successful we must eliminate our weaknesses rather than maximize our strengths. The *Career Distinction* mindset requires that you only be concerned with those weaknesses that will get in the way of your success. Otherwise you should expend your efforts on enhancing your strengths and making them more visible to those around you.

To build your personal brand, you need to know what your strengths are and then use them to achieve your goals. You can augment and validate your 360°Reach results—and thus further clarify your understanding of what your strengths are—by taking the online StrengthsFinder self-assessment developed by Gallup. (*Now, Discover Your Strengths* contains instructions for gaining access to this tool.)

We are all born with wonderful gifts. We use these gifts to express ourselves, to amuse, to strengthen, and to communicate. We begin as children to explore and develop our talents, often unaware that we are unique, that not everyone can do what we're doing!

—Lynn Johnston, Canadian cartoonist

You've gained insights about your vision, purpose, goals, values, and passions through introspection. And you've identified your brand attributes and strengths by finding out how others perceive you. Now you need to identify your brand community—the network of people who most need to know about your brand in order for you to achieve your career goals.

Chapter 6

Define Your Brand Community

In this chapter, you will learn:

- Who comprises your brand community
- How to assess your competitive differentiation
- The importance of your target audience

Before you can deliver clear, consistent, and constant communication about your personal brand (discussed in Step 2: Express), you need to know who you should talk to. Those who successfully plan their careers connect regularly with the members of their brand communities. Your *brand community* comprises all the people who know you and should know you, as shown in Figure 6.1.

Notice that your brand community consists of a series of concentric rings: The people represented in the rings closest to you—that is, individuals who know you best—should know the most about your brand. As you move out from the center, awareness of your brand can be weaker. Your goal is to communicate a consistent and powerful brand presence to all members of your brand community. When they know and understand your brand, they can convey the brand to members of *their* brand communities—thereby further increasing awareness of your unique promise of value.

Team, Family, Friends
Peers
Management, Customers, Business Partners
External Associations
The World-at-Large

Figure 6.1   Your Brand Community

Your brand community consists of the following people:

- *The people who work for you, your boss, friends, and family:* This element of your brand community consists of people who know you best. These individuals should have such great clarity about your brand that they can communicate it to others on your behalf. Why do we include employees in this group of brand-community members? The people who work for you are looking for enlightened leadership. They need to know who you are and what you stand for before they will follow you and generate the business results your team needs. And we include bosses because they are instrumental in helping you achieve your goals. The better they know you, the easier it will be for them to support your career development.

- *Your peers:* You must prove your worth not only to those above you and below you in your organization's hierarchy, but to your colleagues as well. This includes your peers at your current company and individuals in other organizations who share your job function. Gone are the days when you only had to impress your manager or the CEO. Success means consistently demonstrating your value to your colleagues as well. When you do this, you begin to stand out and gain respect and notoriety.

- *Your competitors:* Your peers can also be your competitors—individuals who have the same goals. After all, your resume will be sitting alongside theirs on the desk of your prospective next boss. So in addition to building relationships and a solid reputation with your peers, you must be crystal clear about what differentiates you from them. How can you stand out unless you know among whom you are standing?

If your offering is identical to your competitors', there will be no reason for a potential new boss or employer to select you. Just as consumers make instant decisions to buy Nike over Reebok or to fly jetBlue instead of Delta, you want to ensure that your "customers" pick you over your rivals. And that means ensuring that they know what makes you unique. Often, what distinguishes you from rivals are your brand attributes.

Tip: To determine your differentiating characteristics, go back to the strengths you identified in the previous chapter and observe the strengths of your peers.

To define what makes you different from your competitors, you may find it helpful to first consider your similarities. Two examples follow.

LARISSA, FINANCE MANAGER, FASHION COMPANY

When Larissa analyzed the ways in which she was similar to and different from her peers, she came up with the following lists:

How Are We the Same?
- Degree in accounting
- MBA (Finance)
- 10 Years' experience
- Organized

- Detail oriented
- Ethical
- Dependable

What Makes Me Different?

- Team oriented/collaborative
- 5 Years' experience working in fashion during university
- Interest in fashion
- Trendy and trendsetting
- Hobby in designing jewelry
- Excellent at delivering presentations
- Quick, dry wit
- Confidence

MARCUS, SALES EXECUTIVE,
BUSINESS FURNITURE COMPANY

Marcus's same/different competition analysis looked like this:

How Are We the Same?

- Bachelor of science degree
- 8 Years' sales experience
- Solid communication skills
- Confidence
- Knowledge of office furniture

What Makes Me Different?

- Go the extra mile for clients
- Genuinely care about people
- Not 100 percent focused on making money
- Excellent relationship builder

- Love cold-calling
- Lots of national contacts (have lived in five different states)
- Speak Spanish fluently

- *Management, customers, and business partners in your organization:* In the new world of work, you probably don't work in a silo; you may well be part of a multidisciplinary, cross-organizational project team or task force working toward a single, focused objective. Your worth to your organization increases as you demonstrate the value you can contribute beyond functional, divisional, and geographic boundaries. That's why, regardless of your role in your organization, you need to communicate your brand to people who are in your organization but outside your job function. These individuals include higher-ups who lead departments and functions other than yours, internal customers, and business partners such as external constituencies with whom you regularly work.

- *External constituencies:* Thanks to globalization, it is no longer sufficient to express your brand just within the walls of your company. To succeed today, you must demonstrate that you are a member of the larger community. Increasing your external visibility builds your brand with additional people who can influence your career now and in the future. Moreover, your external connections increase your value to your current organization by the external reputation that you build. We discuss the networking elements of brand community in detail in Chapter 14.

The Importance of Your Target Audience

Your target audience is the subset of your brand community that is *most* critical to your ability to reach your ultimate career goal. And you need to be in constant contact with them. You must start conversations with them—and keep the conversations going. Through these ongoing exchanges, you cultivate the strong relationships essential to achieving your objectives.

> *All men are caught in an inescapable network of mutuality.*
> —Martin Luther King Jr., Civil Rights leader

Companies understand this rule about staying in touch with their target customers. Volvo, for example, sends its message of safety to mothers in every issue of *Working Mother* magazine. The Coca-Cola Company communicates its brand to the whole world a thousand times a day through product placement, billboards, TV ads, vending machines, and consumers sipping from Coke cans as they walk down the street.

As you'll see in Step 2: Express, to reach your career goals, you must practice the "three Cs" of branding with your target audience: (1) Clarity: You express your unique promise of value, (2) Consistency: You always send the same on-brand message through the content and style of your communication, and (3) Constancy: You communicate frequently. When you practice the three Cs, you remain visible to your target audience.

William had an experience that revealed the importance of target audience visibility. He was being interviewed by a radio station in Rochester, New York, just after the announcement of major layoffs at Kodak. During the interview, he spoke about how personal branding can help people survive layoffs. A woman called in and said:

> I'm an extremely hard worker. I come in every morning before everyone else in my department and rarely leave my cubicle during the day. I never leave unfinished work in the evening. I'm conscientious and work more hours than my colleagues, yet I learned yesterday that I will be laid off in the coming weeks. I don't know what I could have done differently. I can't think of many people who work as hard as I do.

As this caller's story shows, hard work is not enough to secure a job in today's business world. Of course, it is an essential first step: You won't get anywhere without being able to produce results. But you need to do much more to remain in the driver's seat of your career. You must ensure that what you do—and how you do it—are constantly visible to those around you. Instead of just being the hardest worker, the caller should have *built a reputation for being the hardest worker*—by regularly communicating her brand to those around her.

We aren't talking about blatant personal advertising. We're talking about constructing a reputation for the qualities that make you unique. Being visible is not shameless self-promotion. It's communicating with members of your brand community so that they understand what distinguishes you.

**Tip: Get others to evangelize your
strengths and accomplishments by communicating
the value that you are delivering to them.**

William had another experience that taught him the power of communication firsthand. He was working on a TV show on personal branding for the BBC in Manchester, United Kingdom, and was the guest expert. If you've ever worked on a TV program, you know that there is a lot of idle time as crew members set scenes, arrange props, and so forth. During such off-camera moments, William and the producer/director, Fiona O'Sullivan, chatted about branding.

One conversation in particular stood out. William was telling Fiona that everything is a brand. He used the Eiffel Tower as an example, explaining that the tower is not only a brand in itself (with its own unique promise of value); it's also the brand *symbol* for France and Paris. "Ask 10 people about the Eiffel Tower," he said to Fiona, "and you'll get similar responses from all of them. That's how strong a brand it is. The Eiffel Tower is perhaps more widely recognized than the French flag."

Years later, William received a call from Fiona. She said she had been asked to direct a new TV program for the Discovery Channel called *The Secrets of the Eiffel Tower*. And she asked William if he would appear at the beginning of the program to introduce it. William's attention to communication had won him a unique opportunity to contribute in a way he greatly enjoys and at which he excels.

Identifying Members of Your Target Audience

Remember that your target audience consists of the people who are in the best position to help you reach your career goals. To identify members of your target audience, think about your career objectives. If your goal is to move up the ranks in your existing company, you may know many members of your target audience by name. For example, Pamela, a marketing executive in a small software company, wants to head up philanthropy in her current company. She has identified the following people as her target audience:

- The current vice president of philanthropy
- The managers in the philanthropy team
- The vice president of human resources
- The public relations manager (who is responsible for corporate social responsibility communications)
- Her current manager
- The CEO of the company

If you want to move to a different industry, function, location, or some combination of the three, you may be unable to identify your target audience members by name. Instead, you might have to identify them by job title as well as other demographic and psychographic data. To identify target audience members by *demographic* data, consider the following criteria:

- Age range
- Gender
- Career/job position/title
- Income
- Location/geography
- Education

To identify target audience members by *psychographic* data, consider these criteria:

- What do they do in their spare time?
- What do they like to read?
- What websites or portals do they visit for information?
- What magazines or newsletters do they read?
- What are their professional activities outside of work?
- What are their volunteer activities outside of work?

Focusing on Your Target

The key to effective branding is focus. Instead of communicating your brand to the entire world, you'll convey it specifically to those who can help you reach your goals. Just as Volvo does not waste resources communicating about safety to 16-year-old boys (who are more interested in speed), you must be clear about who you're going to communicate with. William always says, "Personal branding is not about being famous. It's about being *selectively* famous." The following story offers an example of how one person developed a plan for focusing his brand communication.

KYLE, MARKETING EXECUTIVE, PHARMACEUTICAL COMPANY

Kyle is a marketing executive in a large pharmaceutical firm. Ultimately, he would like to run a major, highly visible account for a large ad agency, and eventually he would like to have his own agency. He identified his target audience members as:

- His team, peers in his company, and his senior management
- CEOs of big pharmaceutical companies
- Ad-agency senior executives
- Marketing executives in general
- Pharmaceutical R&D and new product development managers
- Recruiters who work with marketing executives

Kyle then developed a plan for initiating and maintaining conversations with all these members of his target audience. You'll find more information about his communication plan in later chapters.

Nothing can add more power to your life than concentrating all your energies on a limited set of targets.

—Nido Qubein, business consultant,
author, and speaker

If you are as focused as Kyle, then communicating with your target audience won't be onerous. And that's a good thing. After all, you do have a demanding day job. You have to ensure that enhancing your visibility to your brand community—especially your target audience—doesn't step up your stress. In addition to narrowing down the list of people to whom you'll communicate your brand, you also need to tell your brand story as concisely and compellingly as possible as discussed in the next chapter.

Chapter 7

Tell Your
Brand Story

In this chapter, you will learn:

- What a personal brand statement and profile are and why they're important
- How to craft your personal brand statement and brand profile
- How to use your brand statement and profile to drive your personal and professional decisions

In Chapters 4 through 6, you identified key components of your brand—the attributes that enable you to deliver unique value. In this chapter, you put all those components together in one sentence that describes the value you offer—whom it's intended for and what makes you different. This is your personal brand statement (PBS). You then use your PBS and everything else you have learned about yourself and your motivations to develop a broader expression of your unique promise of value—your brand profile. Both the statement and profile guide your career decisions and put you in a position to express your brand through all of your communications including your resume and "elevator pitch." Together, your PBS and brand profile keep you in the driver's seat of your career.

A PBS can take many shapes. A few examples follow:

MARK: Using my sarcastic wit, understanding of people, and passion for creativity, I empower cutting-edge advertising teams to deliver the powerful, breakthrough advertising campaigns that yield revenue and brand value for consumer products companies.

WILLIAM: I use my 20 years' experience in corporate branding, passion for human potential, and avid pursuit of innovation to inspire and motivate executives, professionals, and entrepreneurs across the globe to achieve the highest level of professional success.

KIRSTEN: I use my energy, forward thinking, and passion for web technology to help high-achievers take control of their own career success.

Tip: Before creating your PBS, go back and review your work in the *Career Distinction Workbook* (www.careerdistinction.com/workbook) and highlight the words that best describe your unique promise of value.

Putting Your Brand Statement to Work

Why create your PBS? It helps you on numerous fronts. You can use it as a:

- *Reminder of your life's purpose.* Your PBS serves as a constant reminder of what you want to do with your life.
- *Compass for making important decisions.* As you progress through your career, you can expect to face a series of daunting decisions—

everything from whether to accept a promotion or job offer to which professional development assignments would be best for you. As much as you might wish for a bell signaling that you have made the correct choice when such decisions crop up, no such bell exists. However, your PBS can serve as a compass to guide your choices. For example, if a manager in another department asked you to consider an open position on her team, you would be able to compare that opportunity against your PBS to see if it fits.

- *Filter for setting priorities.* Your PBS helps keep your brand in the forefront of your mind and thereby serves as a filter for setting priorities. In this way, your PBS enables you to "put first things first" and say no to conflicting demands or commitments that are off-brand for you. For instance, your PBS helps you decide whether you should accept the offer to speak at your professional association's upcoming conference or spend the time finishing the white paper you are writing.

- *Communication tool.* Your PBS communicates in a concise, clear way what you are here to do. It enables you to quickly tell others what value you can offer them. Make it evident to those around you what you can offer them.

- *Chance to maximize your talents.* Talents grow with use, yet many of us are modest about our talents and gifts. Generally our personal brand calls us to use all of these skills and requires that we use them daily for our own benefit and the benefit of others.

- *Opportunity magnet.* When you communicate your brand through your PBS, you attract people who value what you have to offer. And those individuals bring new professional opportunities your way. To illustrate, as Kirsten began speaking exclusively on topics related to career success online, she found that she gained more clients and future opportunities to present.

The story that follows demonstrates the benefits of creating a PBS.

ALLAN LAWRENCE, REVENUE ACCELERATOR
MASQUERADING AS FACILITIES ENGINEER

Allan Lawrence knows that building a career is not about looking for a job. That's why, when he learned about personal branding, he called Deb Dib to assist him in defining his brand.

Allan understood the power of branding from a corporate perspective because his employer was a prominent hotel chain that emphasized branding at every level. Allan embraced the concept and strived to envelop his work and his team in the attributes of the corporate brand. He saw how effective this practice was and wanted to translate that experience to his career.

Deb helped Allan define his personal brand and its value to an employer (Allan's value proposition). Allan's PBS became: "Allan Lawrence is a revenue accelerator, brand evangelist, and customer satisfaction specialist who just happens to be a facilities engineer and manager." For Allan, the brand and the customer experience are intertwined drivers of revenue and profit.

Once Allan defined his passion for branding and its effect on the organization, he felt empowered to ensure that everything around him was sending a powerful on-brand message. He also set out to expand his visibility to additional professional organizations.

He has continued building a reputation at work for being far more than an engineer. In fact, he has become a strategy partner in determining how to integrate the brand direction with the hotel story and a member of his property's core management team—a far cry from the typical duties of a facilities engineer.

Allan has effectively differentiated himself from those around him in his company and industry. If he ever wants to make a change, his career will benefit from his unique brand as much as his company now benefits from his brand-driven management style.

Developing Your Personal Brand Statement

An effective PBS possesses these three qualities:

1. It consists of just one sentence.
2. It can be easily understood by a 12-year-old.
3. You could recite it from memory at gunpoint.

> —*Good things, when short, are twice as good.*
> —Baltasar Gracian, author of
> *The Art of Worldly Wisdom*

Consider these additional examples of PBSs:

SANDIE: I use my quirky nature and my belief in making everything fun to motivate marketing teams to work together more effectively to drive greater value for their organizations. (If I can't make it fun, I won't do it.)

BOB: Sitting at the intersection of technology and business, I use my passion for communication to help IT professionals in Fortune 100 companies express themselves in ways that are understood by businesspeople.

MONICA: I inspire and activate high-achieving salespeople in healthcare organizations through my focus on motivation, positivity, empathy, and competition.

Tip: Test out three versions of your personal brand statement with members of your target audience and trusted colleagues, and see which one resonates with them.

To draft your PBS, go to www.careerdistinction.com/workbook and complete the exercise, Writing Your Personal Brand Statement.

Once you've come up with a rough draft for your PBS, spend some time reworking the draft until it rings true for you. Let ideas roll around in your mind for a while to see how they feel and sound. Don't feel compelled to use this formula slavishly. If you think you can express your brand better through another format, be creative. Your PBS should be unique to *you!*

Also, keep in mind that your PBS is not your promotional tagline—such as Nike's "Just Do It" or Garnier's "Take Care" or the Marines' "The Few. The Proud." Instead, it is a concise summary of how you intend to solve a problem, meet a need, or make a difference in the world. Table 7.1 helps you gauge the effectiveness of your PBS.

Writing Your Brand Profile

Now that you have drafted your PBS, expand it into a brand profile—a fuller summary of your vision, purpose, values, passions, attributes, strengths, and goals. An example appears in the box on page 77.

> If one is the master of one thing and understands one thing well, one has at the same time insight into and understanding of many things.
>
> —Vincent van Gogh,
> Dutch Post-Impressionist painter

You can refer to the brand profile exercise in the workbook at www.careerdistinction.com/workbook.

Your brand profile is a useful tool for developing career-marketing tools—such as your resume, elevator pitch, biography, and Web portfolio copy. We'll cover these in more detail in Chapter 8.

Table 7.1   PBS Checklist

For each statement below, check Yes or No. Then read the instructions for interpreting your score.

My personal brand statement . . .	Yes	No
1. Is inspiring.		
2. Is exciting.		
3. Is clear.		
4. Is engaging.		
5. Speaks to my target audience.		
6. Is consistent with my vision and purpose.		
7. Reflects my passions and values.		
8. Makes me feel proud.		
9. Feels familiar and comfortable to me.		
10. Evokes times when I have felt most fulfilled and engaged in my life.		
Total		

Interpreting your score: If you checked Yes for at least seven of the statements, your PBS is likely very effective. For any statements where you checked No, consider how you might further revise your PBS so that you can honestly respond to the statement with a Yes.

Mark's Brand Profile

Mark is an advertising executive, but not just any advertising executive. He is steadfastly focused on building the most creative and effective breakthrough ad campaigns the world has ever seen. He believes that creativity is *the* essential ingredient in advertising. Creativity makes an ad worthy of remark. And Mark believes that creativity is the soul of any advertising team. It is the spirit that keeps people united, inspires them to greatness, and keeps them going all night to meet a deadline.

- Mark says: Advertising's role is to build a company's brand and its revenue. Creativity is what separates a good ad from a stellar one.
- Mark's Vision: A world where everyone is encouraged to exhibit their creativity for their own fulfillment and the enjoyment of all.
- Mark's Purpose: To empower a high-performing creative team of inspired executives to deliver breakthrough materials that impact many people's lives.
- Mark's Attributes: Creative, witty, sarcastic, collaborative, driven, results-focused.

Putting Your Brand Profile to Work

Once you've completed your brand profile, put it to work. The following guidelines can help:

- *Refer to your brand profile daily*—especially when making decisions about what job to take, which assignment to choose, and how to position yourself in your field. Measure your brand against your employer's brand statement (the organization's mission, vision, and values). Are they compatible with your own vision, purpose, and values?

- *Bring your brand profile home.* How does your brand operate within your home? What can you do to better align your activities outside of work and your brand environment (explained in Chapter 12) with your brand?

- *Give away your brand.* If this is truly what you are compelled to do on this earth, don't make it all about money. How can you add value to the world or your community by living and breathing your brand?

Throughout the rest of this book, you'll frequently use your PBS and your brand profile to communicate your brand to your target audience (Step 2: Express in the 1-2-3 Success! process) and to manage your brand environment (Step 3: Exude).

Now that you've completed Step 1: Extract in our 1-2-3 Success! process, you're ready to move to Step 2: Express. During that step, you will discover more specific strategies for using your PBS, brand profile, and other means to communicate your unique promise of value to your target audience.

EXPRESS—
COMMUNICATE YOUR
BRAND TO YOUR
TARGET AUDIENCE

Express
- Create Your Career-Marketing Tools
- Express Yourself
- Assess Your Online Identity
- Build Your Brand in Bits and Bytes

In Step 1: Extract—Unearth your Unique Promise of Value, you focused on articulating your brand and identifying the people in your brand community. Once you know your brand, your competitors, and your target audience, you can formulate a communications plan for reaching those people who need to know about you so you can achieve your goals. This is the Express phase of the 1-2-3 Success! personal branding process. In Chapters 8 through 11, we show you how to create career-marketing tools, express your brand in the physical world (as opposed to online), and build your brand in the virtual world.

In the Express phase, we also stress the importance of the "three Cs" of branding: (1) clarity (about who you are and who you are not), (2) consistency (in your message about who you are), and (3) constancy (continual visibility to your target audience).

Chapter 8

Create Your Career-Marketing Tools

In this chapter, you will learn:

- What traditional career-marketing tools are and why it's important to brand them
- How to stamp your resume, cover letter, and bio with your personal brand
- How to go beyond what is expected in your career-marketing materials

In communicating your brand to your target audience, you can make use of traditional career-marketing tools: your resume, biography (bio), and cover letter. Of course, in today's business world, you must be in perpetual career-management mode—thus, you should always have ready-to-go, updated versions of each of these tools. However, as we explain in this chapter, you also need to stamp each of these tools with your brand, so that they stand out in the minds of your target audience members. Otherwise, you risk disappearing into the sea of resumes, bios, and cover letters already out there. After all, your resume is likely sitting in a pile or a database among hundreds of your rivals', and your bio is just one among the many circulating on billions of Web pages. By distinguishing yourself through these tools, you gain a vital edge over your competition.

Thankfully, ensuring that your career-marketing tools stand out is a relatively manageable task. That's because most of the tools out there don't come anywhere near reaching their potential. Consider resumes. Our reaction to the vast majority of resumes we read? Yawn. And Kirsten has seen thousands of these, as a former professional resume writer and volunteer reviewer at job fairs. Moreover, most of the bios we see are no more than laundry lists of credentials. Besides being downright boring, many resumes and bios lack focus: Their creators throw in every bit of information they can think up, in the hopes that some of these bits will "stick" in the minds of the people reading them. But readers have neither the time nor the inclination to figure out what you want from them and why you're the most qualified to get it. The minute they sense a lack of focus and clarity on your part, they'll toss your resume or bio in the "circular file" and move on to the next one sitting atop the pile on their desk.

Before you can paint a compelling portrait of your unique promise of value in your bio, resume, and cover letters, you must have invested the necessary soul-searching to determine what separates you from your peers. If you've worked Chapters 4 through 7 (the Extract phase of the 1-2-3 Success! process), you've done at least some of that soul-searching and have developed a personal brand statement and profile. You can use these to apply your brand consistently and concisely across your career-marketing materials. Next, we take a closer look at each tool in your career-marketing arsenal and explain how to stamp it with your personal brand.

It *Is* All about You: Branding Your Bio

To create your career-marketing tools, start with your bio. This tool will be a reference for your other communications and will help you infuse them with color and a personal quality. In a bio, you have more flexibility to let your personality shine.

Your bio can be an excellent career-marketing and networking tool. Savvy executives post their bios on the TheLadders.com (the leading job website for 100K+ professionals) Professional Network and get noticed by executive recruiters there. As these executives have discovered, your career bio—if written well—enables readers to quickly grasp your experience, capabilities, and successes. What are the keys to an effective bio? Avoid the temptation to list *all* your credentials, job titles, and degrees in a tightly packed paragraph. You'll only bore people with this formulaic approach. Kirsten once had to introduce a speaker at the last minute during a conference and was forced to read a dry recitation of the speaker's career history from the bio she had submitted. The recitation utterly failed to communicate the speaker's unique point of view—depriving her of the opportunity to distinguish herself from the many other presenters at the same gathering.

Here's an example of a boring bio:

After graduating from Harvard with degrees in business and psychology, Ellen Smith started her career in consumer packaged goods. Rising through the ranks to become a brand manager, she left consumer goods to pursue business-to-business branding. Now, as the vice president of branding for a major IT company, Ellen draws on her past experience in the consumer arena to drive brand value for her current employer. A member of the American Marketing Association and IT Marketing Foundation, Ellen teaches marketing and branding at local universities.

Does that bio make you want to get to know Ellen? Probably not. After all, it doesn't say anything that makes Ellen unique or communicate anything interesting or exciting about her. In contrast, consider this excerpt from Allan Lawrence's bio:

Allan Lawrence—director of engineering with Marriott's Renaissance Westchester Hotel in White Plains, New York—is not a typical engineering professional. Rather, he is a revenue accelerator, brand evangelist, and customer-satisfaction specialist who just happens to be a facilities engineer and manager. For Allan, the brand and the customer experience are intertwined drivers of revenue and profit.

An executive focused on excellence, Allan has said, "Every touch point of the customer experience should speak to the brand's core values; its mission should be apparent. When a customer can see and experience those values while in contact with the facilities staff or its work, the ultimate result is revenue driven by satisfied customers!"

With a 15-year background driving client satisfaction, Allan Lawrence supports the corporate brand initiative by seeking and establishing operational solutions and processes that prevent reoccurring support costs from "leeching" profits from owners and stakeholders. He strengthens the organizational infrastructure by implementing key strategic business initiatives in business continuity, emergency management, energy conservation, and continuous change management.

Many people reading Allan Lawrence's bio would instantly be intrigued by his claim that he's "not a typical engineering professional," his use of lively quotations, and his active, muscular prose ("leeching profits from owners and stakeholders," "strengthens the organizational infrastructure"). Telling a story can also help you make your bio memorable. Consider this excerpt from the bio of one of Kirsten's clients:

Robert Francisco is a financial marketing director who helps independent business professionals achieve their professional goals by creatively distilling complex concepts into streamlined solutions. A coffee fan who enjoys roasting his own coffee beans, Rob became dissatisfied with how inconsistently other members of his household made the morning brew. He wanted to express to them how to grind the beans for a consistently enjoyable coffee experience. So, one morning, his household awoke to find a sign that he had placed next to the coffee maker. It read, "Respect the bean."

From that day forward, the caffeinated mantra became a sort of guiding philosophy for Rob. Now, Respect the Bean is the name of his blog. Constantly brimming with ideas for businesses, everything that Rob does relates to his desire to maintain authenticity.

> *When we lose the right to be different, we lose the privilege to be free.*
> —Charles Evans Hughes, chief justice of the United States 1930–1941

In Step 1: Extract, you distilled all your insights about your vision, purpose, goals, values, and passions into a one-sentence brand statement. Your bio should begin with your brand statement and then provide the who, what, where, when, and why details that make your story compelling. Write in a style that reflects your attributes, and strive to make an emotional connection with your readers. You want it to attract the people with whom you'd *most* like to work. Your bio is not the place to be conservative and cautious. "A branded bio is about guts," Deb Dib says. "It's the guts to be yourself, the guts to break a mold, and the guts to know that your bio may raise some eyebrows. It's the courage to say, 'Here's who I am. Here's what makes me, *me*. I can't and won't be all things to all people. But I *am* the right person for *this* job.'"

As you work on your bio, get input from others who know you. Ask them, "Does this make you think of me?" Also consider seeking help from a professional writer and testing your bio with hiring managers and executive recruiters. Once you're satisfied with your bio, create versions in different lengths that will work for your Web portfolio, blog, online networking profile (at sites such as LinkedIn or ZoomInfo), and at the end of articles you've written. (We discuss these communications tools in greater detail in Chapter 11.)

Tip: To get inspiration for your own bio, keep track
of bios that you find compelling (at the end of articles,
on websites, etc.) and determine why they stand out.

Crafting the Right Resume

For many human resources departments and hiring managers, the re-sume is still the standard screening tool. Thus, you'll need an up-to-date version of this career-marketing tool at all times—whether you're actively job hunting or happily employed. Most resumes now in circulation present work histories and highlight responsibilities rather than achievements. Therefore, they don't differentiate one candidate from the next. And many resumes are deliberately general: A focused resume, people assume, could exclude them from opportunities they hadn't thought of previously. Yet, this kind of "be all things to all people" thinking isn't congruent with personal branding.

The key to a great resume is positioning yourself for a *specific* kind of opportunity and communicating *only* the information that will be relevant to the people who can give you access to that opportunity—your target audience. Think of your resume as an advertisement for you. You want it to grab readers' attention immediately so they can then digest the rest of the information more thoughtfully. You can use formatting to control where readers' eyes go first when they begin reviewing the document. For example, through the strategic use of bold type, you can emphasize impressive phrases from your achievements, your advanced degrees, and relevant client or company names. Think of your resume as playing a role in the "ACT B" customer-decision process—by which your "customer" (reader) decides whether to eventually "buy" you. Your resume and cover letter serve as tools for increasing readers' *awareness* of you and *consideration* of whether you merit a *trial* (job interview). If the interviews go well, readers will *buy* (hire) you.

Examine the current version of your resume. Ask yourself:

- Is it up to date?
- Is it compelling?
- Is it written in my unique voice?
- Does it communicate my brand message?
- Would others in my field be unable to use it?

If you can answer "yes" to these questions, your resume is on the right track.

As with your bio, you want your resume to net you meetings with members of your target audience. Most hiring managers or recruiters take only 10 to 30 seconds to scan a resume. For this reason, you'll need to write yours in a way that communicates your brand within that short amount of time—and that compels your reader to put you on his or her short list of potential interviewees. You should also craft the resume using relevant keywords so that readers using a database search can easily retrieve it.

To identify the right keywords, search job descriptions and online job postings that are particularly interesting to you. Phrases that are common to *all* these descriptions and postings are the important ones. If the job titles on your resume aren't the same as the one you desire, add your target title at the beginning of your Summary of Qualifications. Or, create a keywords section at the end of your resume for the ASCII text version that you'll post or submit through an online form.

The best way to communicate your brand quickly is to begin your resume with a Summary of Qualifications (sometimes also called a Profile or Executive Summary). To write your summary, review your brand profile and your bio, picking out the main points. Make sure the summary articulates what you do, for whom you do it, and what your strengths are. Weave your primary brand attributes into the copy to convey your work style. In the experience section, include only those jobs and achievements that support your brand *and* are relevant to your career objective. Even though the summary appears first on your resume, you'll want to write it last. That way, you can start with the easiest parts of the document and work up to the summary to tie everything together and position yourself correctly for your target audience.

The following information belongs in your resume summary:

- A heading—such as "Chief Financial Officer—Construction Industry." The heading immediately positions you for a certain level and function—even if it represents the job you *intend* to have, not one you've had in the past.
- Your brand statement in a "tagline" format. For example, "Passionate about Marketing. Focused on Results" or "Driving Innovation through Collaboration."
- The scope of your relevant experience. Summarize what you've done and convey how it positions you for what you want to do now.
- Your core competencies.
- The added value that your background brings to the table, especially if you're seeking to change careers.

According to Wendy Enelow, the author of more than 20 books on executive job searching:

The single most important consideration in resume writing is to create an accurate picture of how you want to be perceived *now* (not in the past). Using your objective as the overall framework for your resume, how can you integrate your experiences to support that objective? You'll find that the answer may not be the traditional chronological resume format, but perhaps a more unique strategy. For example, if you're an EVP of Sales looking for another sales management position, the resume writing process is reasonably straightforward. However, if you're that same EVP of Sales who is now looking to transition into a general management role, your resume will be entirely different. Although you'll continue to highlight your strong revenue performance, you'll want equal emphasis on your management achievements, roles, and responsibilities.

To develop your summary of qualifications, refer to the exercise in the *Career Distinction Workbook* (www.careerdistinction.com /workbook).

In writing the rest of your resume, there are no hard and fast rules—except, of course, perfect spelling and grammar. For example, despite the old adage that a resume should only be one or two pages long, you may go beyond two pages if your content is relevant and interesting. Here are some additional tips for creating a powerfully branded resume:

- Start with your education, community service, and the basic details of your career experience—such as job titles, company names, and dates. For each job, write a very short paragraph summarizing the scope of your responsibilities.

- Reserve the bullet points under each job for your achievements. Demonstrate your solutions to challenges, and note the results you generated for your organization.

- Quantify where possible (e.g., "Delivered $10 million in revenue through an online advertising budget of $500K" or "Led a team of 18 finance managers located in 5 cities throughout Europe and the Americas").

- Begin each bullet point with the strongest action verb that accurately conveys your contribution. Verbs like *initiated*, *spearheaded*, *solved*, *created*, and *led* pack much more of a punch than *managed*, *contributed*, *worked with*, and *handled*.

- Use a chronologically based structure if you are continuing on the same track and your work history doesn't include major gaps. If you are changing fields, organize the information according to function rather than chronology to showcase your transferable skills. Some people who are changing careers also use a combination of structures—listing relevant strengths and achievements on the first page for hiring decision makers and providing the chronological story on the second page for human resource managers and recruiters who want this more traditional structure.

- Delete anything that doesn't position you for your goals or that you don't want to do any longer.

- Only list hobbies, interests, or volunteer work if they are relevant and they validate your skills or strengths or make you much more interesting to hiring managers.

- Remove all jargon and acronyms. Ensure that people who didn't work for your company can understand you.

- Make it easy for people to find you by including a stable physical address, phone, and e-mail address.

- Provide links to your website, blog, or online profile, where people can find evidence of your thought leadership and past performance. See Chapter 11 for more information on building your online identity.

- Ensure that your resume adheres to the standards of the country in which you are applying.

- After writing your Summary of Qualifications, go back and make sure that your experience section completely supports your summary.

- Consider having a qualified professional write or review your resume. Also show it to several advisors (preferably in your target field) for their advice before circulating it.

- Include select endorsements from colleagues or clients. This can be an especially effective technique when you are trying to position yourself for a career change.

- Make the design of your printed resume consistent with your brand identity. We talk more about brand identity in Chapter 13.

- Don't fold your resume. Print it on quality paper, and mail it in a large envelope.

> *People think that I can teach them style. What stuff it all is! Have something to say, and say it as clearly as you can. That is the only secret of style.*
>
> —Matthew Arnold, major Victorian poet

Applying these practices takes time, but the results are worthwhile. Take a look at this client success story from Kim Batson of careermanagementcoaching.com. It illustrates how a powerful personal brand can significantly accelerate your job search, attract the right employers, advance you quickly from the interviewing process to the offer stage, and raise your value (for higher compensation) in the eyes of a potential employer:

DANIEL SIMPSON

With a newly developed personal brand, value proposition, branded resume, and cover letter, Daniel launched his job search. Immediately, he began receiving calls for interviews. Within a two- to three-week period of intense interviewing, he received an astounding eight job offers!

In addition, all the offers were at a base pay increase of $15,000 to $26,000 more than he was making at his current company, including the one he accepted as a director with a $1 billion leader in the industry. This employer moved so quickly to secure Daniel that the entire process from receipt of resume to offer took only four days.

In Daniel's words: "It's not just the resume, but the branding and value proposition that allowed me to consistently advance, differentiate myself, and win. . . . I couldn't ask for better success."

Daniel's Brand Statement: "As a strategic, result-oriented, high-energy federal IT business development executive, I specialize in driving revenue and profits for firms engaged in highly complex technical solutions and emerging technologies. I am passionate about creating customer delight by consistently exceeding my customer's expectations."

Daniel's Core Value Proposition: A 10-year successful track record of selling and delivering highly complex technical solutions to the federal government, inspiring sales and delivery teams to higher levels of performance, and consistently creating customer delight (see Figure 8.1).

To further stand out, consider using appropriate creative approaches to getting your resume in the right hands. If out-of-the-box thinking is a requirement for the type of position you're seeking, "walk your talk" with a nontraditional approach to delivering your resume. For example, suppose you're an event planner. In this case, you might send a beautifully formatted invitation to view

---

Daniel R. Simpson
STRATEGIC IT BUSINESS DEVELOPMENT & SALES EXECUTIVE
Revenue Driver For High-Technology Solutions/Emerging Technologies

7225 Easton Close
Felton, DE 19943
H: (703)555-1234 / C: (703)555-6789
E: dsimpson@app.net

Executive Summary

- *Federal Sales Pipeline Development*
- *Strong DHS Sales Experience and Domain Knowledge*
- *Business & Sales Strategy*
- *PMBOK-based Program Management*
- *Key Account Planning & Management*
- *New Market & Product Launch*
- *High-Impact Top Level Presentations*
- *Budgeting / P&L Control*
- *Creative Partnering Strategies*
- *Staff Recruiting & Training*
- *MS-IST from George Washington University (2002)*

■ **Lifecycle business development and sales expertise** with the unique ability to identify, qualify, pursue, win *and* deliver multi-year, multi-million dollar, technology-based solutions to Federal Civilian Agencies.

■ **Specialist in selling highly complex solutions/emerging technologies** including SOA, CRM, ERP, EAI, e-government, supply chain, content management, and business modernization / transformation.

■ **Performance accelerator** inspiring line and matrixed sales teams to higher levels of performance, pivotal to revenue and profit growth.

■ **Expert relationship builder, communicator, and presenter.** Reputation for developing compelling value propositions that gain buy-in at the C-level and across the organization; ardent passion for delivering customer "delight".

■ **Strategic thinker with keen ability to understand client requirements.** Known for developing creative solutions and strong win themes.

Figure 8.1   Daniel's Summary of Qualifications

your Web portfolio. Since your contacts will likely also need your traditional resume, you can offer the downloadable file in various formats there. You could even have balloons printed with your resume. The possibilities are limited only by your imagination.

Tip: To always have a current version of your resume, keep it on your computer desktop. Every time you complete a major project or when a significant professional event occurs (like a promotion or acceptance of an association board position), update it.

Conveying Your Brand through Your Cover Letters

Cover letters—which accompany your resume—are another opportunity to differentiate yourself. In a cover letter, you can make a connection with your reader—explaining why you are contacting them and how you can benefit them. Since resumes focus more on hard skills, use your cover letter to showcase your soft (people) skills and personality. As with your resume and bio, refer to your brand profile when crafting your cover letters.

Effective cover letters are written for the specific intended reader—whether that person is a new networking contact, the

You can find excellent examples of cover letters in these books:

- Wendy Enelow, *Best Cover Letters for $100,000+ Jobs* (Manassas Park, VA: Impact Publications, 2001).
- Wendy Enelow and Louise Kursmark, *Cover Letter Magic* (Indianapolis, IN: JIST Works, 2006).
- Martin Yate, *Cover Letters That Knock 'Em Dead* (Avon, MA: Adams Media Corporation, 2006).

human resources director of a company, a hiring manager whose advertisement you're responding to, or a recruiter. In fact, you'll want to create four different versions of your letter for each of these reader types. Then you can simply customize the opening and closing paragraphs for the specific situation.

In addition to your cover letter, resume, and bio, the following career-management tools can further help you communicate your brand:

- Executive Summary (one-page version of your resume, primarily used for networking).
- Leadership addendum (provides details on your significant and relevant projects in challenge, action, results format). With this approach, you choose the most rewarding and relevant projects of your career and present them by explaining what the challenge was (the problem that existed for the project to be necessary), the steps that you took, and what the results were.
- E-mail signature (text, design, and typography appropriate to your brand).
- Voicemail message (make sure it's professional and reflects your personal brand).
- Web portfolio or blog (covered in Chapter 11).

A Few Words about Job Interviews

When your branded communications have landed you interviews, be prepared to deliver on your promise of value during these face-to-face encounters. Recall those primary messages that appear consistently in your resume, cover letter, and bio. During each interview, reiterate those messages and tell stories to illustrate your key points. Do your homework by researching the company and your interviewers online and reviewing your resume and brand profile. Practice with others so you can express your personal brand regardless of what questions come up during the interview, and so you can follow up to get offers.

Your investment in consistent and distinctive communications will pay off in the form of hiring managers eager to recruit you. It will also help you determine whether a particular job opportunity is right for *you*. We've included an exercise in the *Career Distinction Workbook* to help you make on-brand career decisions.

The standard career marketing tools that we discussed in this chapter should be familiar to you; but the way you develop and use them is different in the brand-you world of work. By using the techniques that we described, you will be able to stand out from your peers and attract the attention of hiring managers. In the past, these tools alone were sufficient, but no more. As you will learn in Chapters 9 through 11, savvy careerists need to augment traditional career marketing tools with other communications that will increase your visibility and credibility. In Chapter 9, we discuss physical communications tools and in Chapters 10 and 11, we share the secrets of becoming virtually visible.

Chapter 9

Express Yourself

In this chapter, you will learn:

- More about the three Cs of branding
- How to identify the communications tools that are right for you and your target audience
- How to build your physical communications plan

Although each personal brand is unique, they all have something in common: They are confident communicators. In fact, a large number of CEOs maintain that it is their oral and written communications skills that got them to the top. You can't build a must-have brand if your communication skills don't enable you to express that brand with energy and confidence.

So, take a moment to honestly evaluate your communications skills by completing the associated exercise in the *Career Distinction Workbook* (www.careerdistinction.com/workbook). If you identify some areas that could benefit from improvement (such as writing or public speaking), make a plan to strengthen those skills.

Understanding the Three Cs of Brand Communication

Every strong brand in the world can boast three essential qualities: clarity, consistency, and constancy. Next we explain these qualities and provide examples. By understanding the three Cs of brand communication, you can more easily gauge the effectiveness of your own brand communication plan.

Clarity

To have a strong brand, you must be clear about who you are *and* who you are not. You also need to understand what your unique promise of value is and how this promise enables you to attract people who can help you achieve your goals. Richard Branson, for example, is crystal-clear about being a risk-taker. He is not your typical CEO in a conservative blue suit, white shirt, and red tie. Instead, he's a daredevil who donned a wedding gown when he launched Virgin Bridal and went nude when he launched his book *Virginity*. Among his first big, risky ventures was signing the British punk-rock group the Sex Pistols on his record label when no one else would consider them. Now, he is planning to fly people to outer space. Even outside the professional arena, Richard Branson is clear about being a risk-taker, which he demonstrated when he circumnavigated the world in a hot-air balloon.

Consistency

In addition to being clear about who you are, you also must be consistent—that is, steadfastly expressing your brand no matter what communications vehicles you choose. Madonna is an excellent example of brand consistency. She's the chameleon brand of entertainment. She reinvents herself with each CD that she produces. If you're thinking that's not consistency, you're not alone. But in fact, Madonna changes with incredible consistency, each time starting a trend. And only she could produce a sex book and then follow it up with a children's book. Thanks to her consistent changing, Madonna has her public perched on the edge of their seats, waiting to see what she'll come up with next. Her ability to change consistently throughout her career separates her from other entertainers, thereby strengthening her brand.

Constancy

Strong brands are constant—always visible to members of their target audience. Consider Oprah. She never goes into hiding. With her weekly television show, her book club, her magazine, her numerous media appearances, and her casual appearances in grocery stores and restaurants where she lives, Oprah is constantly in view and therefore has become an incredibly strong brand.

Building Your Communications Wheel

As with any other effort you invest to achieve your professional goals, you need to carefully formulate a plan for communicating your brand. We help our clients create such plans by encouraging them to visualize what we call a communications wheel, as shown in Figure 9.1. To complete your own communications wheel, check the associated exercise in the *Career Distinction Workbook*.

The communications wheel enables you to graphically depict your communications plan. As you work through the Express phase, you'll populate your wheel with the communications vehicles that will best help you express your brand to your target audience members. Notice, however, that *content themes*—the key messages you want to get across to your target audience—sit at the center of your wheel and apply to all of the communications vehicles you identify. This is the *clarity* part of the three Cs. Your content themes help your communications stand out and ensure that members of your target audience associate those communications with you . . . and only you.

Content themes also give you an opportunity to take a stand. After all, strong brands aren't wishy-washy. They express firm opin-

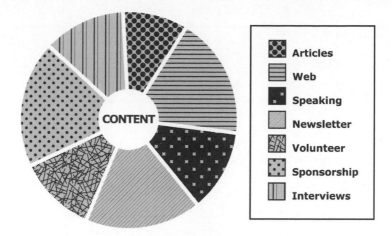

Figure 9.1   The Communications Wheel

ions and make those opinions known. As you've probably gathered, branding is not about pleasing everyone. For example, not everyone is an avid fan of Starbucks like William is. And although Kirsten can't imagine it, not everyone thinks the iPOD is the only MP3 player worth owning. But when you express your brand with confidence, people respect you even if they don't agree with your message.

> *The only thing worse than being talked about is not being talked about.*
>
> —Oscar Wilde,
> Irish playwright, novelist, and poet

Several of our clients identified the content themes that follow:

SALLY, MARKETING EXECUTIVE

Successful marketers take risks. Marketing is all about experimentation. The best marketing campaigns ever were newly created.

IAN, IT EXECUTIVE

IT is not about technology. It's about understanding a business's information needs and providing the tools to get the right information to the right people.

Establishing Your Thought Leadership

Once you know yourself, your competitors, and your target audience, you can identify the right combination of communications tools to increase your visibility and credibility—making you a must-have professional for hiring managers, executive recruiters, and potential clients and business partners. As we've seen, all strong brands are constant—ever visible to their target audience. So your communications plan will need to include a lot more than traditional career-marketing tools (such as your resume). You'll also need to communicate your thought leadership—by expressing your point of view and demonstrating your expertise through your *communications mix*—the different communications vehicles you choose to use. Your communications mix can vary widely, depending on your goals. For example, William's goal for Reach is to be the global leader in personal branding. To do that, he needs to work with a lot of people across the globe. So he has developed a communications mix including public seminars to large audiences, webcasts that can be viewed in real time and on-demand (to account for different time zones), and publicity in international publications, like *Time*.

Whatever you include in your communications mix, be sure to achieve a blend that appeals to you *and* that enables you to reach your audience. For example, suppose public speaking is a great way to reach your audience, but it scares you to death. In this case, you must either master your fear or find another way to reach your audience. Conversely, if you enjoy writing e-newsletters but your target audience is made up of CEOs, you may want to consider another communications medium that CEOs are more likely to read, such as articles published in magazines like *Fortune* or *Forbes*. Finally, if writing articles or a book is the best way to reach your audience but you don't enjoy writing, consider hiring a ghostwriter or getting help from someone in your network who loves to write. Expanding on your professional success should be fun and interesting. So don't make it hard on yourself by designing a communications mix that doesn't excite you. The goal is to communicate your brand with ease. Remember, the exciting part of personal branding is that it helps you achieve your goals while simultaneously increasing your personal and professional satisfaction.

In addition to using your communications mix to establish your thought leadership, you can leverage your intellectual property (IP)—that is, the ideas you've come up with about a particular topic. Indeed, IP is "it" when you're seeking to differentiate yourself. When you develop your ideas such that others associate them only with you, your IP becomes a critical brand asset you can use to demonstrate your thought leadership.

> *There are no new ideas, There are only new ways of making them felt.*
>
> —Audre Lorde, poet and activist

We know this firsthand. We didn't invent branding or personal branding. But we do have strong ideas about how best to *use* personal branding. William has a passion for human potential and 20 years of branding expertise. And he greatly enjoys helping careerists achieve personal and professional success. He has combined these passions to develop the unique three-step process described in this book. He uses this structured and proven methodology to differentiate himself from the numerous other personal branding consultants that are scattered across the globe.

That's his IP. Kirsten similarly has used her expertise in the career-management industry, her understanding of technology, and her Reach certification to develop a unique system for building powerful brands online.

Developing Your Physical Communications Plan

Your physical communications plan consists of activities such as public speaking or writing articles for a magazine or newspaper. We call this your physical communications plan to differentiate it from your online communications, which we discuss in detail in Chapters 10 and 11. Your physical plan can vary widely, depending on your goals and your target audience. However, you stand a greater chance of implementing your plan if you list specific communications activities along with a time line for carrying them out.

> *Good communication is as stimulating as black coffee—and just as hard to sleep after.*
>
> —Anne Morrow Lindbergh,
> pioneering aviator and author

To develop your communications plan, consider the physical communications tools you have available to you.

Speaking

Use public speaking to enhance your visibility and communicate your brand. Even if you don't choose public speaking as part of your brand communications plan, be sure to develop some proficiency in this area. After all, professionals at all levels of an organization are asked at times to deliver presentations to a variety of audiences. And presentations are most effective when they're authentic—delivered with your true voice, your personal brand. By mastering the basics of making presentations, you'll express your authentic personal brand convincingly and effectively to audiences.

Tip: The best way to overcome the nervousness that often accompanies public speaking is to get plenty of practice with this skill. The more you do it, the more comfortable you'll become at it. So volunteer for every possible speaking opportunity. And consider joining a public-speaking practice group, such as Toastmasters.

Public speaking is an excellent way for people to experience your brand. By listening to and watching you, your audience gets *all* of you. You can express your brand through the words you choose, the tone and pitch of your voice, your facial expressions, and your posture. And you can use multimedia presentation tools, such as PowerPoint, to enhance and reinforce your message. Delivering a presentation to an audience gives you the greatest opportunity to communicate your passion, demonstrate your expertise, and convey your personality.

If you *do* include public speaking as one of your communications tools, volunteer for speaking opportunities within your company or at professional or volunteer organizations. Search the Web for information on upcoming conferences, and submit proposals to requests for presenters. Most conferences select speakers between 3 and 12 months in advance of the event. With some careful planning, you can fill your speaking calendar for the coming year. Remember to make all proposals you submit relevant to the event theme. Ensure that your topics are timely and, of course, consistent with your brand.

Writing

Publishing is no longer just for professors. In the new world of work, getting your ideas in print is vital to enhancing your career prospects. Writing articles and white papers that state your position on an on-brand topic enables you to get your brand in front of your peers, your boss or client, and (ideally) your next boss or client. The story that follows shows the advantages of publishing articles—whether in print or online.

SCOTT DAVIS, SENIOR PARTNER, GLOBAL BRAND CONSULTING FIRM

Scott Davis has been building his personal brand for the past 14 years by integrating a combination of expertise marketing activities—from teaching at Kellogg and writing two books to chairing major conferences around the world and writing a monthly column for *Advertising Age*. He realized early on that his *Advertising Age* articles weren't just about reaching the magazine's subscriber base: They could serve as a powerful networking tool.

Scott writes these articles of interest for both chief marketing officers and CMO wannabes. The articles give him an opportunity to reach out to his personal network of more than 1,500 marketers as well as to his company's overall database of more than 13,000. He has a built-in chance to further strengthen his personal network through a few mouse clicks each month.

The column has helped Scott to connect with past contacts, clients, friends, students, colleagues, and potential new clients on a regular basis. Several new projects, as well as new hires, have come his way as a result of his column. As a "lucky strike extra," he often gets to feature past clients in his articles—strengthening those relationships even further.

How do you find the right publications for your brand? Discover which magazines and professional journals are featuring stories relevant to your brand by checking out their editorial calendars. Most publications post their editorial calendars on the Web. You can also contact the periodical directly. Read a few issues of the magazine before writing your article, to familiarize yourself with the type, length, and tone of the articles it accepts.

Tip: When reading trade journals and other professional publications, note editors' and journalists' names and contact information. That way, you can submit story ideas or volunteer to contribute expert insights to their articles.

In addition to writing for publications, think about the many ways you can further promote your personal brand through the written word. For example, you might write for your company's internal newsletter or contribute articles to local community and professional organizations. Publishing—in a wide variety of places—increases your visibility and highlights your strengths.

Also consider writing a book. Of course, this can be a major endeavor (as we know from firsthand experience!). But being a published book author further bolsters your credibility and differentiates you from many of your peers. There's an old adage that says everyone has at least one good book in them. If you feel compelled to write a book, talk with others who have done so to gain insights into how to approach the work, how to prepare a book proposal and shop it around to publishers, and other related tasks.

Remember to save copies of every written piece that you've had published, along with information about where each piece was published. That way, you can build a complete portfolio to support your brand.

Colors fade, temples crumble, empires fall, but wise words endure.

—Edward Thorndike, American psychologist

Participating in Organizations

Another way to express your brand is to take an active and visible role in a professional or philanthropic organization. Choose a role that enables you to express your brand through speaking, writing, designing programs, and so forth. You'll generate much more of an impact by selecting a few organizations and taking a leadership role in them than by spreading yourself too thin across many organizations. Serving on a board will especially help you forge strong connections with the organization's membership.

If you have difficulty identifying a professional or philanthropic organization that appeals to you, start one. Founding an organization is hard work, but it goes a long way to building your visibility, credibility, and network. We examine the importance of professional associations and your network in further detail in Chapter 14.

Getting Creative

In addition to using the traditional physical communications tools just described, be creative. If you can find an interesting and original way to reach your target audience, all the better. Consider the following story about a professional who developed her own programs directly connected to her unique promise of value.

PATRICIA HUME, VICE PRESIDENT,
BUSINESS PARTNERS AND ALLIANCES

Pat is an empathetic leader who collects loyal fans wherever she goes. Her warmth and openness, her respect for people, her ability to motivate others around a single effort—all of these qualities differentiate her from her peers and inspire loyalty among those who work for her. When she moves from one part of an organization to another, people line up outside her door in hopes of making the same move.

Pat is completely open and honest with others—a rare trait not shared by most of her colleagues. Indeed, her candor is a major element in her unique promise of value. She "tells it like it is"—but in a way that enables her listeners to hear and appreciate her message.

Pat uses many traditional communications tools to express her thoughts on the importance of communication. She often speaks publicly about the role of communications in motivating teams. In addition, she has invented some communications tools of her own to further express her brand. For example, she developed "Chat with Pat" to foster open communication among her business-partner community (the people who make up her customer base). All members of this community can call in and listen to an honest update on what's happening with the Business Partner Program and ask questions about how the company is doing and how the partners are driving the business. Pat also invented the now-famous "Chug and Hug" events, which took place every Friday on the balcony outside her office. These events were designed to support open and direct communication within her team. Members came together to meet over a beer—and to talk, laugh, vent, share, get to know each other, and, yes, hug.

Tip: Be lazy. It's good for your brand. Once you have finished creating a presentation or writing an article, ask yourself how you can re-use it, cut it down into a list of tips, expand the content into a book, and so on.

Executing Your Physical Communications Plan

Once you have identified the physical communication tools you want to use, research each tool to find the best channels through which to deliver your message. For example, suppose you've decided to write articles so as to reach your ideal clients. Find out which magazines, newsletters, and trade journals are appropriate for your message *and* are read by members of your target audience.

Next, prioritize your communications activities, and schedule them in your calendar. An example of Kyle's communications plan follows (Note that some of the activities listed in this plan relate to building an online identity which we discuss in Chapter 11.):

- Schedule speaking engagements at the two primary pharmaceutical marketing conferences.

- Host an internal meeting with all my peers before every new ad campaign my team launches.

- Write one article or have three quotes in *Advertising Week*.

- Volunteer to write a regular column for the local *American Marketing Association* newsletter.

- Coauthor (with an advertising executive) a book about the role of honesty and humanity in pharmaceutical advertising and marketing.

- Host an Ad Agency Roundtable at an upcoming local business event.

- Publish regular articles in marketing portals such as MarketingProfs.com.

- Create a blog where I can regularly post my thoughts on current pharmaceutical advertisements and build a community of like-minded professionals.

- Create a personal website showcasing my career successes and increasing my search-engine visibility.

- Contact journalists who work on advertising stories (in pharmaceuticals).

- Submit book reviews at Amazon.com for all newly released advertising books.

- Regularly post comments on advertising-related blogs.
- Take a board position in a local philanthropic organization.
- Update my bio in a witty style.
- Get a professionally taken headshot.
- Become a member of MENG, the marketing executive's network.

Tips for Developing an Effective Physical Communications Plan

- *Get the most "bang for your buck."* Your goal in building your communications materials is to develop content once and apply it to all the communications vehicles you've identified in your wheel. Developing content in this way has two benefits: First, you get to reuse content, getting the most "bang" for your content-development "buck." Second, you create consistency—one of the most important Cs in personal branding. If you develop your content once and then tailor it slightly for each medium, you'll deliver a consistent, clear message regardless of the medium you're using. For example, one of William's clients is an expert in Search Engine Optimization (SEO). She has created a white paper called the "Ten Rules for Effective SEO." She turned this into a PowerPoint presentation that she delivers to all new members of the IT and marketing departments. She has also written an article by the same name, and she has written 10 subsequent articles—each one covering one of the 10 rules in greater detail. So you can see, all of her content from these communications came from the original white paper. The moral of the story: Be lazy, it's good for your brand.
- *Get comfortable with repeating yourself.* When communicating with your target audience, you need to feel comfortable with repetition. It takes a while for anyone to connect with your message. After all, that message lives among all the other communications that are being thrown at people each day. When you make a commitment to expressing your brand message to a

Table 9.1 Your Communications Plan Checklist

Use this checklist to determine the effectiveness of your communications plan. For each statement, check Yes or No to indicate whether you agree with the statement. Then read the instructions below to interpret your score.

Statement	Yes	No
1. Each element in my communications plan clearly expresses my brand.		
2. Overall the plan is consistent with the key messages I communicate through my brand.		
3. The plan will enhance my thought leadership.		
4. The plan will ensure that I'm constantly visible to members of my target audience.		
5. My plan contains a mix of communications tools.		
6. I feel comfortable carrying out every activity listed in my plan.		
7. I enjoy doing the activities listed in my plan.		
8. For activities in my plan that I feel are important to do but that I'm not yet comfortable doing (e.g., fear of public speaking), I have steps in mind for increasing my comfort level.		
9. I will be able to reuse content I've created through several of the communications vehicles I've identified in my plan.		
10. I've established a timeline for accomplishing every task listed in my plan.		
Totals		

Interpreting your score: If you answered Yes for most of the statements, your communications plan will likely prove effective. For any statement to which you responded No, consider how you might address that weakness so that you can genuinely answer Yes.

specific target audience, don't be fickle. Stay the course with your message—and don't be afraid to repeat yourself. William says he is going to write a country music song and call it *Don't be changin when you should be samin*.

- *Be yourself.* Whether you are giving a presentation or writing a report, make sure you put your brand attributes into it. If you are visionary and future focused, ensure that your presentation reflects those qualities by using the latest technology. If you are passionate and determined, make your communications reflect those traits as well. Give yourself permission to put your personality into everything you communicate.

Your Communications Plan Checklist helps you gauge the effectiveness of your plan (see Table 9.1). Once you get in the habit of communicating regularly with your target audience, you'll soon begin seeing results—in the form of interest in what you are doing. Like-minded professionals will gravitate toward you, and those who know you will be better able to communicate your brand message to others on your behalf. You will see the fruits of your labor in the deeper relationships you build with the members of your brand community. Your reputation will expand, and you will find yourself on the fast-track to your ultimate career goal.

But developing and implementing your physical communications plan isn't enough in itself. You also need to understand and build your online identity. Chapter 10 turns to this subject.

Chapter 10

Assess Your Online Identity

In this chapter, you will learn:

- Why your online identity matters to your personal brand
- How to assess your current online profile

In the new millennium, if your ears are burning, it's not because people are talking about you. It's because they're Googling you. And they are the people who matter: Hiring managers. Executive recruiters. Colleagues. Clients. Business partners. Indeed, the Web has now replaced traditional research resources and is often the first place people go for information on individuals of interest to them—putting the phone book and the reference librarian on the endangered species list. How you are presented on the Web can therefore make or break your efforts to communicate your brand, express your differentiation, and achieve your career goals.

In this chapter, we take a close look at this development and explain how you can use the Web to further enhance and communicate your brand to your target audience.

Eighty-two percent of candidates expect recruiters to look them up online.

—*BusinessWeek*, June 26, 2006

The Age of Google

It's no secret that Google is the world's leading Internet search tool. People in virtually every country in the world use it more than 200 million times a day. But we're not talking about the noun Google; we're referring to the verb. One of the world's newest verbs, "to Google," has become part of everyday vocabulary *and* activity. Many people Google more often than they do any other task while at work each day.

Googling: v. The act of learning about someone or something by performing a Web search.

The first time we heard someone use *Google* as a verb, we were on a conference call with a group of colleagues discussing a new offering we were about to launch. Someone explained that a competitor of ours was "certainly the perceived leader in delivering this type of offering." But another colleague jumped in: "Apparently not. I just Googled her, and almost nothing came up."

Perhaps one of the more visible examples of this new trend came with the popular HBO TV series *Sex in the City*. In an episode during the last season, Sarah Jessica Parker's character, Carrie Bradshaw, spoke with Charlotte about "Googling the Russian" to get more information about him. Regardless of pop-culture or business-world events that fuel this new trend, Googling is far from a fad. It's here to stay. This type of search provides crucial information that people use when making judgments about those around them. The box that follows, "Startling Facts," sheds additional light on the phenomenon of Googling.

As personal brand strategists, we are intrigued by the power of this new phenomenon to help people build and manage their personal

Startling Facts

- A recent Harris Interactive poll showed that 23 percent of people search the names of business associates or colleagues on the Internet before meeting them.[a]

- 77 percent of recruiters Google candidates, according to a 2006 survey by ExecuNet. And 35 percent of recruiters eliminate candidates based on what they find in Google.[b]

- According to comScore, Google continues to increase its share of the search market in the United States. 44.7 percent of all U.S. searches were performed on Google in June 2006.[c]

- Classes are available to help human resource professionals conduct online searches for information on job candidates.

- Recruiters are reviewing profiles of job candidates on sites such as Friendster and ZoomInfo. In fact, 20 percent of Fortune 500 companies seeking candidates use ZoomInfo, a service that automatically creates profiles from aggregated professional information found online.

- A new startup, ReputationDefender, will contact website owners on your behalf to request the removal of content that compromises your reputation.

- If you are meeting with a customer, applying for a new job inside or outside your company, or running for a board position, you can count on being Googled.

[a] InfoSpace Press Release, "Web Users Beware: Personal Online Activity May Pose Professional Risk; Survey Shows U.S. Adults Search Online for Information about Colleagues, Employees, and Customers," October 21, 2004, http://investor .infospaceinc.com/ReleaseDetail.cfm?ReleaseID=166008&PageSection=PressRoom.
[b] ExecuNet Press Release, "Growing Number of Job Searches Disrupted by Digital Dirt," June 12, 2006, http://www.execunet.com/m_releases_content.cfm?id=3349.
[c] comScore Press Release, "Google's U.S. Search Market Share Continues to Climb in June; Yahoo! Also Posts Gains," July 18, 2006, http://www.comscore .com/press/release.asp?press=935.

brand. Think about it: Being Googled reveals how visible you are on the Web, and visibility (at least among your target audience) is critical to successful career management. Your Google results powerfully influence those seeking to make decisions about you. So the prospect of being Googled brings up some interesting questions if you are building and nurturing your personal brand:

- If you don't show up in a Google search, do you exist? In this age of online searches, you are "somebody" if your Google results cover multiple pages. By contrast, you are an unknown brand if an online search engine can't find you, or worse, if it finds your name only in a list of obituaries. So if you don't show up in cyberspace, will the person researching you simply dismiss you?

- Will being Googled replace reference checking in job interviews and client bids? After all, online search engines provide a much more objective view than those whom you select to serve as references for you. Will your Google results be the determining factor in whether you get to see a new client or are considered for a job?

We don't have all the answers to these questions. But we *do* have valuable ideas for how you might use, strengthen, and express your personal brand online. First, however, you need to determine your current digital profile—your assessment of how well information on the Web communicates your personal brand.

Accenture included the total number of relevant Google results as one of three measures they used to develop their list of the Top 50 Business Gurus.

—Accenture's website, *Outlook Journal,*
January 2003

Determine Your Current Digital Profile

What does your current online identity reveal? Right now, open a new browser window, go to Google.com, type your name into the search box, and see what the world's most popular search engine says about you. Surprised? Delighted? Depressed? Embarrassed? Do you have digital dirt—that is, information about you on the Web that could negatively impact your career? If Googling your name results in inaccurate or inadequate information about you, you're going to have to correct the situation by creating a Web presence that communicates your personal brand. And you need to get your website to rank higher in the search engines than information that you don't want people to see.

Tip: Type your name in quotes (like this: "William Arruda") in your browser to get the most accurate results.

Perhaps your Google results don't convey the image you want to share with the world. That was the case for Susan, a marketing executive who had been fired by the board of her company. Her company posted the meeting minutes detailing her firing on the Web. When anyone performed a Google search using her name, the first item displayed was the summary of those meeting minutes. She didn't understand why she couldn't get any job interviews—until an executive recruiter told her about her Google results. Before that, she had no idea she had been "digitally dissed."

The moral of the story? Google yourself regularly. To those who don't know you personally, you *are* your Google results—no matter how inaccurate or unfair those results may be. Finding out what Google says about you (also called ego-surfing) is important and influencing what Google reveals is essential. According to *BusinessWeek*, 33 percent of job candidates have never Googled themselves. Maybe some of them are having the same unpleasant experiences Susan had. If you're looking to advance in your career, you'll want to proactively manage your online identity to ensure stellar online-search results.

> **Tip:** Every Monday morning, Google yourself and keep track of any changes in your results.

Figure 10.1 shows four potential scenarios for your online identity. The *y* axis represents the volume of information about you on the Web. The *x* axis depicts the relevance of that information to your personal brand. (Specifically, does the information say what you want it to say? Is it consistent? Does it help people understand who you are and what you stand for?)

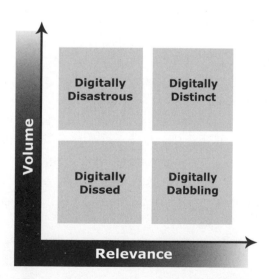

Figure 10.1   Online Identity Matrix

How do you determine the volume of information generated by a Web search on you? First eliminate results that are not about you. To do this, count the total number of entries on the first three pages of your Google results. Then count how many of these results are actually about you. (Some of them may be about other individuals who have the same name as you.) Divide the number of results that are about you by the total number of results on the first three pages. Then multiply this number by the total results Google yielded (in the upper-right corner of the results page). This gives you a good approximation of your volume of *accurate* results—those that are about you. For example:

Of 20 total items on the first three pages, 15 were about me, so:

$$\frac{15}{20} = 0.75$$

$$0.75 \times 1,100 \text{ total results} = 825 \text{ accurate results}$$

In researching thousands of professionals—including CEOs, independent consultants, celebrities, entry-level job seekers, thought leaders, and university students—we've developed the benchmarks in Table 10.1 so that we can help you evaluate your search results volume.

In addition to having the appropriate volume of accurate search results, you need to ensure that those results are *relevant*—that they clearly communicate your personal brand and position you to achieve your goals. Obviously, you want your results to communicate your unique promise of value. Table 10.2 shows how to rate the relevance of your results.

What's your volume of accurate results? And how consistently do those results communicate your personal brand? Based on your evaluation of these two criteria, determine which of the following profiles best describes your current online identity:

Table 10.1   Evaluate the Volume of Your Search Results

If You Are . . .	Number of Accurate Results You Should Have
A professional with 0–5 years' experience (e.g., you're a very recent university graduate).	5–50
A professional with 5–10 years' experience.	50–500
A director-level people manager with over 10 years' experience, an independent consultant, or a small business owner.	500–5,000
A vice president, acknowledged thought leader, highly regarded consultant, or subject-matter expert.	5,000–50,000
A corporate-level executive at a major company, a highly acclaimed consultant or expert, or a best-selling author.	50,000–500,000
A celebrity, an internationally acclaimed guru, or a politician.	More than 500,000

Table 10.2   Rate the Relevance of Your Search Results

If . . .	Your Search Results Have . . .
Most/all of the results are not about you (but are about someone with your same name), or they refer to things that have no relation to your area of expertise.	No relevance
Most of the results are not about you or refer to things that have no relation to your area of expertise, but some do communicate your area of expertise.	Little relevance
About half of the entries are about you and express your area of expertise, and there are many references to your website or blog.	Some relevance
About three-quarters of all entries are about you and express your personal brand.	High relevance
Almost all of your results are about you and are very consistent with your area of expertise and how you want to be known.	Complete relevance

- *Digitally disguised:* There is absolutely nothing about you on the Web. Your search—"firstname lastname"—did not match any documents. It doesn't mean you don't exist, but it means that you remain hidden from those who may be researching you.

- *Digitally dissed:* There is little on the Web about you, and what *is* there is either negative or inconsistent with how you want to be known.

- *Digitally disastrous:* There is much information about you on the Web, but it has little relevance to what you want to express about yourself. The information may also include Google results about someone else who shares your name.

- *Digitally dabbling:* There is some on-brand information on the Web about you. Although the volume of results is not high, the material that's there is relevant to your personal brand. This is an easy fix.

- *Digitally distinct:* There are lots of results about you and most, if not all, reinforce your unique promise of value. Though this is nirvana in the world of online identity, remember that your Google results can change as fast as the weather in London. The lesson? You need to regularly monitor them to see if they need correcting.

> *The [past] 10 years have seen everything from the rise of online Job Boards to the Brand Called You, the birth of blogs to offshoring. All of these developments have had a significant impact on the way we manage our careers— and the next 10 years promise to be just as dramatic.*
>
> —Fast Company, March 2006

No matter what your digital profile is, you can always improve it. By steadily expanding your online presence and increasing your visibility and credibility, you put yourself directly on the path to digital distinction—and you remain distinct even as information about you changes in cyberspace. Of course, you can't build an online reputation unless you first articulate your unique promise of value—your brand. And communicating your brand is especially challenging online, since your presence will be among billions of other Web pages and people click away from sites quickly—the moment they decide that it wasn't what they were seeking. Therefore, before you attempt to build or reshape your online identity, make sure you're comfortable with and confident about the work you did in Chapters 4 through 7, the Extract phase of our 1-2-3 Success! process.

> *Promoting yourself online is the best, easiest, fastest way to build your personal brand.*
>
> —Boris Mann, "Web 2.0 and
> Personal Brand Development"

Chapter 11

Build Your Brand in Bits and Bytes

In this chapter, you will learn:

- How you can use online identity tools (such as blogs and your personal website) to build your brand
- Ways to create content to enhance your online presence
- The dos and don'ts of building your online identity

Now that you have a clear understanding of your baseline online profile, you can develop a plan to enhance it. To craft the right Web identity for your brand, you have numerous options at your disposal. You can maintain a blog, create a professional website, use online networking sites, and develop on-brand content by publishing online articles and participating in web-based communities. If possible, you should try to do all of these. When you use these tools wisely, you cultivate a Web presence that ensures you'll show up in search results the way you intend. Next, we explain how to use such tools to build your brand in bits and bytes.

Join the Blogosphere

A blog (derived from the term *Weblog*) is a chronological online, regularly updated, record of a person's thoughts and commentary about subjects of interest to him or her. Unlike message boards, most blogs have one author (or a few authors). Interestingly, more and more professionals and corporations are maintaining blogs. In fact, there are 100,000 new blogs launched each day, according to blog tracker Technorati (*Time*, November 2006). Blogs are the most economical way for you to create an attractive, on-brand Web presence without having to be a programmer.

> *Blogs will become the new must-have executive accessory, just as e-mail is today. They amplify any senior executive's communications from one-to-one to one-to-many.*
>
> —Debbie Weil, author of
> *The Corporate Blogging Book*

Blogs are an excellent platform from which you can promote your personal brand online—to build both visibility and credibility. By creating a leading-edge, well-organized blog that is related to your niche or area of expertise, you further differentiate yourself from all those professionals who seem to do what you do.

> *My blog is my primary career communications medium because it reinforces my personal dynamism and change-agent brand attributes, illustrates my use of technology to achieve results, and differentiates me in a crowded technology marketplace.*
>
> —Nina Burokas, brand strategist

By inviting comment from visitors, blogs also create an interactive community—and all strong brands solicit feedback and two-way conversations with their constituencies. Blogs improve your search-engine rankings (meaning they help ensure that you appear at the beginning of lists of results), too, because ranking algorithms value frequently updated content. In fact, some people active in the "blogosphere" proclaim that blog is really an acronym for Better Listing On Google.

To easily start a blog, go to any one of these leading hosted blogging applications and follow the instructions for setting up your account and configuring your content:

- www.typepad.com
- www.wordpress.org
- www.blogger.com

If you aren't a Web programmer, we recommend TypePad's Plus Level because it allows for your own branding and customization while still being user friendly.

What to Write

If you want to establish a job search or career-management blog, what should you write in it? There are no rules, but common sense and good writing principles apply. Also, make sure the blog's content focuses on professional matters. Most blogs used for job searching include not only downloadable resumes and professionally focused posts but also irrelevant personal information, such as the blogger's favorite foods or movies. That mix can quickly turn off a hiring manager.

If you are currently employed, familiarize yourself with your company's blogging policy. If you closely associate your personal brand with the company's and are helping to build the organization's brand through your blog, the company could make a move to own your blog if you leave. So, consider blogging about your overall function and the industry, but not your employer.

We recommend using most of your blog posts to establish your thought leadership on a particular topic or group of related topics. The key to a stand-out blog is to own a niche and find your authentic voice for commenting on that niche. You might focus your posts on your specialized competencies, the concerns of your target audience, or your unique way of delivering value to your audience. Figure out an overarching theme for your posts' content. Then, make sure that each post fits neatly under that theme.

> *Blogs allow you to stop hiding behind a stilted/stifled brand and allow you to show up fully engaged with a warmer, more authentic personality.*
> —Andy Wibbels, author of *Blog Wild*

People expect your blog to reveal your personality, so provide a small window into your world as well. Think about interests you might include on a resume that are noteworthy and supportive to your candidacy. Then apply the same criteria to any personal content on your blog. Your blog should not look as if a robot developed it. Instead, it should reflect your personal brand attributes.

Tip: If you want to blog about personal stuff that could have a negative impact on your career, consider setting up your blog at www.vox.com, which maintains your privacy by giving you the ability to control the content that is for the public Internet versus your own private network.

Care and Feeding of Your Blog

The biggest challenge in creating a blog is posting regularly enough to justify this medium. One question we hear often is, "How frequently do I need to post?" It's an understandable concern in an age when most people are busy enough with other responsibilities. Blogging experts maintain that three times a week is ideal. However, this frequency is not practical for most people. We recommend once a week and definitely not less than twice a month. If you can't commit to blogging at least twice a month, you may want to use other tools instead to build your online identity.

Tip: To get inspiration for writing your blog posts, use a newsreader, like Bloglines, to subscribe to online syndicated content. Also subscribe to Google News Alerts (http://www.google.com/alerts) using the keywords that relate to your niche.

Create a Web Portfolio

Developing a website can be the best way to create a controlled, on-brand presence online without having to constantly generate new content. With a Web portfolio, you can provide a comprehensive picture of who you are professionally and what your relevant accomplishments are.

When we use the word *portfolio*, we're not talking about oversized black leather cases with zippers that secure three of the four sides. We're talking about cyberspace. A Web portfolio is the traditional paper portfolio concept reinvented for the online medium, with links and multimedia content. For example, if you're a marketing executive, your Web portfolio might contain your brand bio, case studies, links to press coverage of your initiatives, audio testimonials, and a video clip of your recent presentation for the American Marketing Association. Portfolios are more than Web-based resumes in that they contain tangible evidence of your professional achievements.

Like the creators of any other website, you want your Web portfolio to attract traffic—something you can accomplish, in part, by ensuring that the site is easy to use and inviting to the eye. Because many Web-based career "portfolios" are poorly designed, you have a valuable opportunity to further impress visitors by ensuring that *your* site looks polished and professional. You've probably noticed that a lot of websites intended to support their creators' careers look amateurish. Many also mix personal information (religion, politics, lifestyle) and family photos with career-related content. Or, they provide no information beyond what's already in the person's resume. Avoid these gaffes, and you differentiate yourself from others even further.

Tip: Before including any content in your Web portfolio, ask yourself if your manager, potential employer, or customer would approve.

Proving Your Mettle

In a Korn/Ferry online survey, 44.7 percent of respondents said they believed that resume fraud among executives is increasing. Web portfolios protect you from being seen as fraudulent by enabling you to provide evidence of your achievements, not just tell visitors about what you've accomplished. For example, if you claim to have strong presentation skills, you can show a video clip on your website. Articles, awards, white papers, press releases, and schedules of speaking engagements are just some of the additional ways in which you can prove your expertise. Lance Weatherby shows his expertise with click-and-play Flash video clips of his interviews on CNBC and Tech Now. Figure 11.1 provides an illustration.

Through your website, you can also provide tangible, multimedia evidence of your ability to follow through on your promise of value. Once you've fostered virtual rapport with visitors by supplying this evidence, your telephone or in-person meetings will begin at a

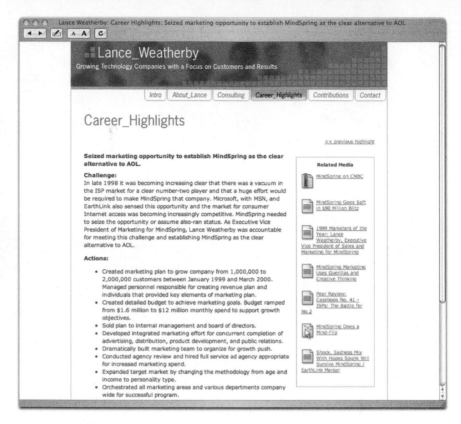

Figure 11.1   Multimedia Proof of Performance

deeper, more productive level. And it helps you weed out no-win situations by revealing more about you earlier in the evaluation process. For example, Alexandre Guéniot's singing Flash CV (www.flashcv.com), which contained an on-brand presentation, netted him an internship at Microsoft. A creative approach like this certainly wouldn't work for everyone. And that's the point. What would work for *your brand?*

Of course, people are busy and want to quickly find information about you online. Thus, it's always better to be clear than clever in how you design your website. After all, hiring managers don't have time to figure out how your skills and experiences *might* benefit them. You have to tell people, in straightforward terms, exactly *what* you want to do for them and *why* you're the most qualified to do it. That's why clarifying your brand must always precede your Web-development efforts.

So, how do you grab visitors' attention quickly online—and keep it? A clear brand statement/tagline, compelling design, and easy-to-navigate information architecture are keys to keeping visitors on your site long enough to want to learn more.

Heather Henrick's Web portfolio design and content reflect her creativity and passion for pushing the limits—whether it be in her work, volunteer activities, or adventurous outdoor pursuits. Her area of specialty is immediately evident in her tagline. See more at www.heatherhenricks.com (Figure 11.2).

Figure 11.2   Capturing Interest Online

Creating my Web portfolio is, without question, one of the best career moves that I've made. Executive recruiters frequently call me with incredible opportunities even while I've been happily employed.

—Heather Henricks

Carefully consider the design and layout of your website. Even if the content is well written and compelling, the wrong design—one that doesn't reflect your brand—will only work against you. For instance, if your brand says "trustworthy financial planner," you wouldn't want your site to look too creative or quirky. Before you build your site, know which brand attributes you want the site to reinforce. If you are unsure about your authentic brand attributes, get some input from those around you with the 360°Reach personal brand assessment that is included with this book. And if you decide to hire a website development company to design and build your site, take care that you select a good one. The box on the facing page offers helpful tips.

Use Online Networking Sites

If for whatever reason you don't want to or can't create an on-brand Web portfolio or blog, you can use online networking sites to post your profile, make connections, and research people and opportunities. Depending on the service you use, you may be able to create a public Web page or minisite based on the template provided by the service. Online networking sites include:

- www.linkedin.com: This by-invitation site is regarded as the premier business networking site and enables you to create a public profile that can be found by search engines.
- www.ryze.com: At Ryze, you can add your photo and connect with others who share similar interests.
- www.ecademy.com: Globally oriented and based in the United Kingdom, ecademy also offers in-person networking events.

- www.zoominfo.com: You may already have a profile at Zoom-Info, because it uses technology to crawl the Web for professionally focused content about you, including those in your network. Check ZoomInfo to see if your profile exists among their 33+ million profiles—and if it is accurate.
- www.ziggs.com: Ziggs is a search engine for corporate bios. It also lets you create your own Ziggs profile (minisite using its template).

Selecting a Website Development Company

A low-quality website is worse for your brand than no website at all. Unless you are a Web designer, get support from the experts. The following criteria can help you choose a Web-development partner:

- Ensure the right skill mix. Does the company have a team comprising individuals skilled in personal branding, career management, design, writing, and Web technologies?
- Verify their multimedia experience. Any service worth its salt should offer audio, video, Flash, blogs, podcasts, screencasts, optimized PDFs, and so forth. Ask to see examples of sites using each technology you are considering.
- Ensure that your provider understands Web usability rules and tests your site.
- Avoid any service that suggests having audio that automatically plays when your portfolio home page loads because they have no clue about job-search etiquette.
- Remember: Technology for technology's sake is pointless. When it comes to video, no one wants to watch a talking head hyping a site or bragging about himself.
- Ask if the company can provide Search Engine Optimization (SEO) services to better position you in search engines.

When you have your own website, you can provide links to it through online networking sites. You can also cross-promote your networking profiles on your site to enhance your online identity. Be sure to revisit your online profiles every few months to make sure they are up to date. Also, don't expect online networking sites to be replacements for actual, face-to-face networking. Instead, they are meant to augment traditional networking. You can get the most from online networking sites by using them to gather your existing network in one place—which gives you easier access to your contacts' networks by making them transparent to you.

Extend Your Brand Online

In addition to developing your own website and blog and having a profile at online networking sites, you have numerous other opportunities to build your online presence. To become digitally distinct, you want to ensure that there's a great deal of content on the Web that consistently expresses your personal brand. Here are some ways to generate that content:

- *Publish:* Publishing articles online about your passions and interests is a great way to increase your visibility during a Google search. There are many article banks and Web portals that will accept your articles. ArticleAnnounce (a Yahoo! Group), for example, takes articles of all kinds and makes them available to those who need content for magazines and e-zines. Find the right places to post your articles, and regularly submit content that will drive members of your target audience to your website or blog.

- *Post:* Post your reviews of books that are relevant to your area of expertise at Amazon.com, barnesandnoble.com, and other online bookstores and provide links in the reviews to your website or blog. But remember: If your area of expertise is nuclear physics, posting a review of your favorite cookbook will only dilute your brand message.

- *Participate:* Join professionally oriented online forums and information exchanges such as Yahoo! Groups or Google Groups. By sharing your expertise, you increase your visibility at the same time. You'll also start to build your brand community with others who share the same interests.

- *Pontificate:* Comment on other people's blogs that are relevant to your personal brand. Get mentioned on others' websites and blogs. Linking with other like-minded individuals improves your Google ranking and further increases your visibility.

Start Now

We find it curious that Web-based portfolios and career management blogs haven't already become the standard. After all, people check in for flights, order groceries, and manage their money online. Why not use the Internet to advance your career as well? Regardless of the industry or job function you're seeking, a blog and website provide similar benefits. But now is the time to master these and other online-identity tools: Once everyone has a website showcasing their accomplishments, it'll be that much harder to make yours stand out. Start now, and you boost your chances of grabbing plum jobs before someone else does. In addition, you will forge positive relationships with new colleagues—as the following story reveals.

> In the future, [employers] aren't going to advertise job openings anymore. . . . They'll find you.
>
> —Fast Company, March 2006

CINDY ENG, PUBLISHING EXECUTIVE FOR CHILDREN'S BOOKS

Cindy Eng was recruited for a senior editor position at Scholastic at Home because a networking contact saw her Web portfolio and referred her. But when her soon-to-be new colleagues learned that she had accepted the position, they expressed concern about the fact that someone new would be joining the division. The group had recently undergone some restructuring, and employees were change weary. To find out more about Cindy, they Googled her name. Thankfully, what came up first in the results was Cindy's Web portfolio—the contents of which increased Cindy's colleagues' confidence about her ability to step in and assume her new responsibilities. Cindy told us, "I think it set their minds at ease that their new boss knew what she was doing."

Dos and Don'ts of Building Your Online Identity

- *Take a stand.* Strong brands have something to say, and they say it with passion and conviction. If you build a me-too site, no one in your target audience is going to pay attention to it. The goal is to stand out—not to blend in. But don't be *too* controversial. You don't want to alienate everyone.

- *Steer clear of dirt.* Avoid visiting and commenting at sites that contain questionable material. You leave a virtual fingerprint everywhere you go. Don't build an online identity that could come back to haunt you.

- *Go for quality over quantity.* If you can invest only a small amount of money and time in your website, go for one or two pages with quality images, stellar copy, and easy navigation.

- *Make the link.* Ensure that all of your online content—your postings, articles, comments, reviews—point back to your website with your contact details. And don't forget your call to action. For example: "If you enjoyed this article about ethics in accounting, sign up for my monthly newsletter, or join my online forum where we regularly discuss ethical issues in finance."

- *Build up your Web content over time.* If the thought of generating all that Web content overwhelms you, break the effort down into more manageable pieces. Remember: If you publish one online article every other month, you'll have six by the end of the year—a decent compilation. With everything you write, shoot for quality. One page of Google results that leads visitors to a series of high-quality experiences with your brand will propel people to take the next step to learn more about you.

- *Be consistent.* To build a solid reputation, you must be known for something, not a hundred things. So build your online identity around who you are and what makes you relevant and compelling to *those people who need to know about you.* Don't try to be all things to all people. When you're clear and consistent, the right people will find you on the Web.

- *Watch your mouth.* Be careful about what you put in your blog. Badmouthing your current employer or revealing corporate information could get you sacked.

- *Call in the professionals.* If you don't have the skills to build a quality website or blog, get someone who can. This is an investment in your career. When it comes to managing your reputation, don't skimp.

- *Lead with your strengths.* Use your creativity, understanding of your subject area, communications skills, and other strengths to showcase your professional prowess online.

- *Show 'em your mug.* Get a professionally taken photograph that exudes your brand. Please note that we said professionally taken—not something you take with your webcam. A high-quality headshot speaks volumes about your brand.

With the advent of Googling, the days of the resume as the sole career-management tool are over. The energy and care that you put into creating a branded online identity just might be the tipping point between you and the other qualified candidate jockeying for the same position or client. In addition to the suggestions offered in Chapters 8 and 9, building your online brand is a key part of Step 2: the Express phase of our 1-2-3 Success! process. Now it's time to move to Step 3: Exude, which focuses on how you can best manage your brand environment.

EXUDE—MANAGE YOUR BRAND ENVIRONMENT

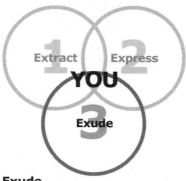

Exude
- Be On-Brand in All That You Do
- Get a Visual Identity
- Increase Your Career Karma

Up to this point, you have uncovered the brand that is you, and you have built a plan to communicate your brand message to everyone who needs to know about you. Now, in the Exude phase, you will make sure that everything that surrounds your brand is sending a consistent on-brand message. The Exude phase is important because it supports brand consistency. When everything about you and around you sends the same on-brand message, you position yourself clearly in the minds of those who will make decisions about you. In this phase, we work on "packaging" you, but as we have said throughout this book, the package must be authentic. In the Exude phase, we focus less on what you do and more on *how* you do it.

143

Chapter 12

Be On-Brand in All That You Do

In this chapter, you will learn:

- How to identify all the components of your brand environment
- How to establish your personal style
- How to develop a plan for making your brand environment consistent with your unique promise of value

In Chapters 8 through 11, you explored Step 2: Express in our 1-2-3 Success! process—a step that focused on communicating your brand to your target audience. This chapter turns to the subject of how to manage your brand environment, which consists of the activities you carry out, the objects in your surroundings, and the people with whom you associate. Your brand environment comprises elements of your appearance (such as your clothing and accessories as well as voice and body language), your office and business tools (including PDAs and briefcases), your brand identity system (the colors, fonts, and images that you use consistently), and your professional network. All of these things say something about you—and thus communicate a message about your brand.

Managing your brand environment means aligning the elements in that environment in ways that reinforce your brand message—your unique promise of value. Strong brands ensure that everything that they do and all that surrounds them—the technologies they use, the clothes they wear, the way they speak, where they conduct business meetings—communicates their brand message.

Corporations also manage their brand environments. Consider Apple Inc.: This organization is all about "thinking different." Apple applies this brand mantra not only to its products, but also to its packaging and retail outlets. If you've ever visited an Apple store, you probably saw instantly that the store was unlike any other electronics or computer retailer. Everything in the place—from its open, clean layout to its Genius Bar—trumpets Apple's signature message: "Think Different." Apple's campus in Cupertino, California, also proves just how different the company really is. Smoothie bars in the cafeteria, hardwood floors, a bring-your-dog-to-work policy—all of these elements encourage employees to "think different" and to deliver on the corporate brand promise.

You Are What's Around You

To be effective, your brand environment must be comfortable for you *and* appealing to your target audience. For instance, if your brand is all about "style and contemporary design," you might decide to meet with a potential new client in the lobby of a W Hotel instead of a more traditional hotel, and to wear stylish attire rather than the more conservative business suit. That's what we mean by aligning your brand environment with your brand.

> *You are a product of your environment. So choose the environment that will best develop you toward your objective. Analyze your life in terms of its environment.*

*Are the things around you helping you toward success—
or are they holding you back?*

—W. Clement Stone, businessman and
advocate of positive mental attitude

Your brand environment communicates your brand even when you aren't there, for example, when someone goes to look for you in your office, even if you aren't sitting there when they arrive, they are forming an opinion of you from what they see. The question you must ask yourself is: How much is my brand environment helping me move toward my goals—or preventing me from achieving them? Note, though, that managing your brand environment doesn't have to mean perfect consistency among every element in that environment. You may have strategic reasons for displaying some inconsistent behaviors. For example, William's accountant John (not his real name) is remarkably skilled at his profession. But his working style is the opposite of the organized, detail-oriented, and buttoned-down manner many people expect from an accountant. When William first saw John's office, he was shocked. Mounds of files teetered on the desk; papers lay strewn across the floor, some of them stained by coffee rings. John says he does his best work under these relaxed, informal conditions but that he realizes he also needs to instill confidence in his clients. His brand—what makes him successful—centers on knowledge, confidence, and flawless execution. Thus, he holds client meetings at the swank little coffee shop around the corner, rather than in his office. In this way, he manages his negative brand attributes and ensures that his clients' interactions with him are always on-brand.

Tip: For the next two weeks, observe everything you do, every tool you use, every article of clothing you wear—all the objects that surround you and all the activities you carry out during a typical day. Ask yourself what each of these objects and activities says about you. If they're saying anything you don't intend, how might you change one or more elements in your brand environment so that they are more on-brand?

Understanding Your Brand Environment's Components

As stated, your brand environment comprises four key components:

1. Appearance
2. Office and business tools
3. Brand identity system
4. Professional network

When you align all these elements so that they work together, you create a symphony that trumpets your personal brand. And that symphony is music to the ears of hiring managers, customers, peers—whoever makes up your target audience. If you neglect to align these elements, you create a cacophonous message that confuses those around you who can help you advance your career. In the sections that follow, we examine the first two elements of your brand environment: your personal appearance and your office and business tools. Chapter 13 explores your visual brand identity system, while Chapter 14 shines the spotlight on your professional network.

"First Impressions Last": Your Appearance

When you meet someone for the first time, that person forms an instant impression of you. If you want him or her to change that impression, studies show that it will take an additional 18 encounters. Clearly, making the *best* impression at that first meeting is critical. Aligning your appearance with your unique promise of value reinforces your brand message for that initial encounter. If you are creative, quick-witted, and dynamic, your appearance must reflect these qualities, for example, by dressing more colorfully or always wearing a different signature accessory. Likewise, if you are conservative, fastidious, and methodical, your clothes and body language need to communicate those attributes. Your apparel, gestures, posture, and movements all communicate something about you.

In addition to being on-brand, your appearance needs to be appropriate for your target audience. A vice president at Right Management, a talent management and outplacement consultancy, told us about a well-qualified executive client who was interviewing for C-suite positions. Every suit he had looked like it had not been dry-cleaned in years. He was extremely competent, had an Ivy League degree, and had a proven track record of growing companies. However, his "rough around the edges" business wardrobe distracted and disturbed the board members who interviewed him. He got many first interviews but seldom made it to the second round. Unfortunately, he apparently had forgotten the maxim "Nothing succeeds like the *appearance* of success."

Tip: Think of your wardrobe as a marketing expense. If you were a business, you would easily spend thousands of dollars on a professionally designed and printed marketing brochure to impress prospective clients. Your clothes and accessories do the same for your personal brand.

In evaluating your appearance, consider how you might use trademarks. Trademarks make you memorable. Think about Elton John—with his thousands of pairs of colorful eyeglasses. Or Steve Jobs, who always wears a black polo shirt with jeans. We're not recommending that you *develop* a trademark, but we *are* suggesting that you flaunt any trademark you have. For example, Sue Brettel, a Reach Certified Strategist, uses her love of the color purple to make herself memorable. Purple stands for creativity and mystery according to color experts—two of Sue's personal brand attributes. No matter what she is wearing, you can be assured that one element or another will be purple—a blouse, a scarf, a pin. Sue also carries around purple folders and a purple briefcase. People associate her with the color.

Your trademark need not be an article of clothing, an accessory, or a color. It could be a phrase that you use all the time or the way you walk. William used to work with a woman who took phrases that were invented elsewhere and made them her own. For example, "What's special about this product that you can't find on the other side of the net [from our competitors]?" "Let's get the space-shuttle [high-level] view of this situation for a minute." In every meeting she attends or presentation she delivers, she uses many such phrases. Others in her company have started using them and attributing them to her. And when they do, they help extend her brand even further. It's like Martha Stewart's, "It's a good thing."

> *Style is knowing who you are, what you want to say and not giving a damn.*
>
> —Gore Vidal, American novelist, essayist, and playwright

Your Office and Business Tools

According to a study by psychologist Samuel Gosling and his colleagues at the University of Texas, people are "remarkably accurate" at guessing one another's personality by looking at their work spaces.[1] Your office, desk, and business tools provide a potent opportunity to reinforce your brand attributes.

When William arrived at his new office at Lotus in Cambridge, Massachusetts, he saw immediately that his surroundings were not on-brand for him. In his office were two desks, each shaped like an L. The room faced the Charles River and Boston skyline. But even with the impressive view, the space wasn't consistent with William's brand. It was impossible for him to hold meetings there. Yet, one of his most prominent brand attributes is "collaborative": William rarely works alone.

One night soon after he started the new job, William removed one of the desks from his office and replaced it with a round table surrounded by four chairs. He also placed a large bowl of Granny Smith apples on the round table. (William is also passionate about fitness; he wrote a book called *Health without the Health Club*.)

These changes made his office more functional *and* communicated his belief in teamwork—an entirely appropriate message in a company whose tagline was "Working together."

Tip: Review all the items in your office—from furniture and carpeting to office supplies and lighting. Ask yourself whether they reflect your brand. What one change would make your office more on-brand?

The story that follows provides an additional example of how one person changed her office to better communicate her brand.

SUSAN, BUSINESS DEVELOPMENT DIRECTOR

Susan had seen firsthand how surroundings can make an impression on colleagues and managers. Her goal was to run her company's European operations. She knew that she would be competing with people who were already working in Europe. But she had a major hurdle to jump: No one associated her with the brand attribute of "global." When she did her 360°Reach assessment, she was the only who checked off the attribute "international." Yet, Susan has extensive international experience. She lived for several years in the United Kingdom and in France, travels extensively outside the United States, speaks three languages, and reads incessantly about foreign cultures. Being global was her best-kept secret.

To ensure that people viewed her as global, she set out to alter her surroundings at work. She put her company's print ads from other countries on one of the walls in her office. She bought four inexpensive clocks, labeled them New York, London, Paris, and Hong Kong, and hung them on another wall. She had her Italian newspaper delivered to the office instead of to her home. And she listed her restaurant and hotel recommendations for several European cities on the company's intranet. In short order, people began thinking of her as Ms. Global, and she is well on the way to achieving her goal.

It's not just the items in your office that shape what people think about you. Every business tool you use sends a message, including communication and organization technologies. What kind of phone do you carry? What's your ring tone? Do you have a paper calendar or a Palm Pilot? What does your screen saver say about you? Consider what your chosen technologies communicate about your brand, and don't underestimate these tools' power.

One reason Kirsten was pegged as technology master at the Career Masters Institute (now The Career Management Alliance) is that she was taking notes at one of their conferences with a PDA and foldable keyboard at a time when those tools were novel. When she was preparing to deliver a presentation at a different conference, she learned that the organizers had planned to provide overhead projectors for the presenters. Kirsten knew she had to purchase an LCD projector out of her own pocket, or her career technology presentation would be completely incongruent with its delivery method. Had she stuck with the provided equipment, the audience would have immediately questioned her technological expertise. Kirsten also brings a remote to easily forward her slides and animations (even if a laptop and projector are provided). Sporting her own remote sends the message that she's a seasoned presenter who's comfortable and familiar with the latest technology.

Whether you're giving a presentation, participating in a meeting, or writing a report, never leave your brand behind. Always ask yourself how you can express your brand more clearly in every situation. Consider the following example.

BRIAN, PUBLIC RELATIONS VICE PRESIDENT

Brian links everything he does to his brand. With his background in public relations, he is a master of the written word. He uses this power to differentiate himself from other public relations executives. For example, when he writes thank-you notes to his team, his colleagues, and partners, he uses an old-fashioned typewriter. This may seem a little odd for someone who does most of his communication through e-mail. But for Brian, it captures his passion for words and communicates his brand attributes of "concern for others," "appreciation," and "creativity." His typed notes differentiate him from other public relations executives and senior executives in his organization, who send thank-yous through e-mail or handwritten notes.

Now that you're more familiar with how to use your appearance as well as your office and business tools to reinforce your brand message, let's turn to another important element of your brand environment: your visual brand identity system. The next chapter explores this subject in detail.

Note

1. The University of Texas at Austin, On Campus, "The Personality of Personal Spaces—Your office or bedroom can reveal more about you than you may think," April 3, 2002, http://www.utexas.edu/opa /pubs/oncampus/02oc_issues/oc020403/oc_personality.html.

Chapter 13

Get a
Visual Identity

In this chapter, you will learn:

- The benefits of having a brand-identity system
- The components of your brand-identity system
- How and where to use your brand-identity system

As a key part of Step 3: Exude—Manage Your Brand Environment, you need to develop and use a customized brand-identity system. Think of your brand-identity system as the visual vocabulary touting your brand. You build the system by selecting on-brand typography, artwork, logos, taglines, and layout standards for all your printed and online career-marketing tools. To consistently send the same message about your unique promise of value, you apply your brand-identity system across all of your communications vehicles (stationery, website, and so forth). This is another area where few people make this kind of effort, which gives *you* even more opportunities to grab your target audience's attention.

If you work for a company, you will need to follow that organization's corporate-identity guidelines in some of your communications.

However, your *overall* identity is not defined solely by your current job. Thus, we suggest creating a separate brand identity system for your personal brand that you'll use for activities such as networking, volunteering, attending professional association events, publishing articles, and creating your website. Your brand identity system enables you to express your brand visually so that you can convey your brand attributes and ensure you are memorable.

Developing Your Identity System

If you are not a graphic designer, work with one who can translate your unique qualities into an on-brand design that will resonate with your target audience. To facilitate the process with your designer, we recommend that you write a design brief similar to this one for a Web portfolio:

Project Title: Web Portfolio for Dawn Little

Background: For over 20 years, within Fortune 500 companies and the Big Four, Dawn has transcended the numbers to orchestrate profitable integrated strategies, turnarounds, and systems conversions. Dawn is currently seeking a senior role in a forward-thinking company with a mission requiring enlightened and strategic leadership complemented by a practical focus on productivity and profit.

Objectives: Create a website that communicates Dawn's brand as a "holistic business strategist" in a way that will be relevant to her target audience: decision makers in print/broadcast media or management consulting. Demonstrate that she is an unconventional CPA.

Scope: Website home page and subpage design. It's likely that the design will be translated into stationery upon approval.

Usage: This website will be used to establish Dawn Little's online identity and provide more information about her unique value. It will include proof of performance to reinforce Dawn's credibility and methods for contacting her.

Format: Navigation is preferred across the top of the page and it will be:

- Intro
- About Dawn
- Career Highlights
- Experience
- Credentials
- Contact

Content that is common to all pages:

- Dawn Little
- Holistic Business Strategist

Include this brand descriptor as a graphical element on home page: Transforming the traditional CPA "bean counter" mentality into a vital business strategist role that serves the whole organization.

Brand Attributes (from 360°Reach analysis): Vision, creativity, pragmatism, execution, analysis, passion, ethics, humanity, tenacity, communication, flexibility, experience, standards, poise, wisdom, dependability, intelligence.

Not all of these attributes can be communicated in the design. Focus on flexibility, creativity, execution, passion (use of color?).

Style: Dawn enjoys color and her favorite is purple (blue shade). She doesn't have font preferences and is open to your expert recommendations.

Imagery: Dawn is getting a professional headshot taken for her About page. She doesn't want her photo to be a major element in the overall design. She prefers photography to illustration.

Legacy elements: There is no preexisting brand identity system.

Timing: Deadline to present first design round is October 11, 2006.

To see the outcome of this design brief, visit www.dawnlittle .com.

In your design brief, you might also include your budget and information about your competition (e.g., URLs of their websites). You can also point to websites of any kind that seem to you to have desirable attributes. Your designer may already have a process for gathering this type of information from you. If so, follow his or her lead. If you've managed design projects in your professional life, you'll simply apply that experience to managing the development of your brand-identity system. If you haven't, we provide an overview of the primary design elements later. You'll want to determine the deliverables you will require from your designer, as well as the order in which he or she will create them. For example, sometimes a logo design dictates the design of your website and stationery. In other cases, your website will be designed first, then your designer can adapt it for use in your blog and stationery. Find out from your designer how many design options and rounds of review and revision will be included in his or her fee.

> *An image is not simply a trademark, a design, a slogan, or an easily remembered picture. It is a studiously crafted personality profile of an individual, institution, corporation, product, or service.*
>
> —Daniel J. Boorstin, American historian, professor, attorney, and writer

Now, let's take a closer look at the elements of good brand-identity design.

Color

Talk with your graphic designer to determine colors that are appropriate to your brand. Color evokes emotion and strong brand recognition. Consider UPS's tagline "What can brown do for you?"

as well as its ubiquitous brown trucks and the brown uniforms its drivers wear. According to color expert Jacci Howard Bear, brown connotes steadfastness, simplicity, friendliness, and dependability—perfect attributes for a logistics company. Through its use of color, UPS closely connects these attributes with its brand promise. Brown is also a highly differentiated color. Can you think of another organization that uses brown as much as UPS does?

Some organizations and even *people* are so steadfast in their use of color that they seem to *own* that color. Think about Home Depot's big, blocky orange letters, the Breast Cancer Awareness movement's use of pink, and performance artist Prince's use of purple. Some companies actually *do* own their colors. Tiffany, for example, has registered its trademark robin's-egg blue as a brand asset. Most people, upon being handed one of those small blue ribbon-tied boxes, would instantly recognize they were receiving a gift from the renowned jewelry company.

Other organizations and products have colorful names. Take Orange (the European telecommunications company), jetBlue, Green Mountain Coffee Roasters, the Red Cross, the Yellow Pages, and Blue Cross/Blue Shield. They all benefit from the power of color to communicate brand attributes and ensure memorability.

Choosing a color to represent your personal brand can be challenging. Table 13.1 shows the attributes associated with specific colors and provides examples of organizations or products that have used those colors. To get ideas for selecting your own colors, review the list and think about which brand attributes you want to emphasize.

> *When we build a website for an executive, one of the key decisions has to do with color. What color or palette of colors will support the client's personal brand attributes and set an appropriate emotional tone—in the way that music colors movie titles?*
>
> —Brian Wu, Brandego founding
> partner and design director

When William worked for the software company Lotus, the firm's hallmark color was not just any yellow, but a custom color called Lotus Yellow. This unique shade was so important to Lotus that the Creative Director, Vartus (a strong brand herself), went to tremendous lengths to ensure that it was used properly on everything associated with Lotus—from brochures to signage to coffee mugs.

Lotus's marketing department also used the color to express the brand internally. From accounting to product development, employees considered how to include some yellow in their day-to-day activities. For example, human resources painted the entire conference room in which orientation was held Lotus Yellow, thus using the color as a powerful and unifying force among all members of the company's brand community.

To generate additional ideas for how you might make the most of color, complete the associated exercise in the *Career Distinction Workbook* (www.careerdistinction.com/workbook).

Table 13.1   The Meaning of Color

Color	Associated Attributes	Organization/Product Logo Examples
Yellow	Bright, positive, warm, visionary, future oriented	DHL, Lotus Software, Hertz, McDonald's
Blue	Credibility, trust, authority, loyalty	IBM, Wal-Mart, Nokia, Ford
Red	Power, risk, excitement, aggressiveness, desire, courage	Coke, Adobe, Target, HSBC
Green	Environmentally friendly, fresh, natural, calming, healing	Starbucks, The Body Shop, British Petroleum, Garnier Fructis
Purple	Luxury, mystery, royalty, wealth, spirituality	Federal Express, Sofitel Hotels, The Church of England
Orange	Determination, energy, vitality, strength, productivity	Hugo Boss, Orange, Home Depot

Typography

If you already have one or two fonts (typefaces) that you like and use consistently, ask your designer if these are appropriate for your target audience. Your designer can guide you in the various personalities and connotations of different fonts. Most fonts fall into two major categories, serif and sans serif. Serif fonts, which have small decorative lines at the ends of the strokes of the letters, are generally viewed as classic. Times New Roman is one example. Sans serif fonts, such as Helvetica, are seen as more modern and clean. Figure 13.1 shows examples of serif and sans serif fonts.

Many people use creative, display fonts for prominent elements in their brand-identity system, such as their logos or website banners. Serif fonts are typically used for body copy in printed materials, while sans serif typefaces are often used for online copy be-

SANS SERIF

Egad, fonts!
News Gothic: solid, reliable

Egad, fonts!
Myriad: contemporary, efficient

Egad, fonts!
Stone Sans (italic): friendly, dynamic

Egad, fonts!
Futura: refined, stylish, creative

Egad, fonts!
Kabel: creative, unconventional

Egad, fonts!
Swiss Rounded: fun, bold, casual

SERIF

Egad, fonts!
Times Roman: trustworthy, versatile

Egad, fonts!
Jenson: intellectual, old-school

Egad, fonts!
Bodoni: stylish, sharp, modern, formal

Egad, fonts!
Galliard (italic): dynamic, classical

Egad, fonts!
Century (italic): friendly, witty

Egad, fonts!
Clarendon: strong, hard-working

Figure 13.1   Sans Serif versus Serif Fonts

cause these fonts are easier to read on a computer monitor. To learn more about the principles and practices of font selection, see *The Non-Designer's Design Book* by Robin Williams (Berkeley, CA: Peachpit Press, 2003).

Images

The strategic and consistent use of images can help you connect with your target audience on a visceral level. For example, the Reach websites always use photographs of people to reinforce the message that we are all about *personal* branding. Depending on what you are trying to communicate and to whom, you and your designer can select photos or illustrations in color, black and white, or decide on some other treatment for images (such as sepia-toned illustrations or photos treated to lend a granular texture or pixelated effect).

In personal branding, *you* are the brand. So, also consider incorporating a photo of yourself in your design. If you have friends who are professional photographers, ask them to take photos of you in your various brand environments to showcase your personality and relevant interests. Or hire a photographer to create the photos. If you're not comfortable with including a photo of yourself in your brand-identity system, by all means don't do it. In fact, one female freelance writer we've worked with was advised by her website designer not to include a photo of herself on her site. Why? Her appearance wasn't relevant to her work, the designer explained. Moreover, as an unfortunate sign of the times, some photos have attracted unwanted comments or attention from site visitors.

Still, many people appreciate being able to connect a face with a name. If you decide to use your photo in your brand-identity system—particularly your website—you can create a deeper connection with members of your target audience *if* you provide the *right* professional photo. Your headshot can inspire confidence and trust and gives you yet another opportunity to exude your brand.

Of course, your photo should be taken by a professional. Resist any temptation to use the snapshot your mother took of you at last year's family picnic. And talk with your photographer about the brand attributes you want your photo to communicate. Make sure he or she takes a range of images you can evaluate before selecting the best one. Show the most promising ones to trusted colleagues, friends, and family members, and ask for their input. And consider something other than the usual headshot (e.g., a full body shot) if it supports your brand and/or the way the photo will be used in layouts.

As Brian Wu says, "The perfect photo is made up of a good pose, good subject styling, good lighting, thoughtful background, good composition, and good cropping." To find a photographer who can provide you with this level of quality, view work samples from potential candidates and consider asking colleagues to recommend photographers they've found to be highly competent.

Once you have your headshot, consider posting it in these career-marketing tools:

- Your website.
- Your virtual network profiles (Ryze, ecademy, and so forth).
- Your articles, ebooks, white papers, or reports.
- Your instant messaging and Skype profiles.
- Your e-mail signature.

Tip: If you are attending an event where there is a professional photographer present, ask if you can get a headshot taken.

Figure 13.2 is an example of good use of professional photos.

Background Patterns and Textures

Many printed and online designs contain layers of elements. Our colleague Myriam-Rose Kohn, who can deliver her international

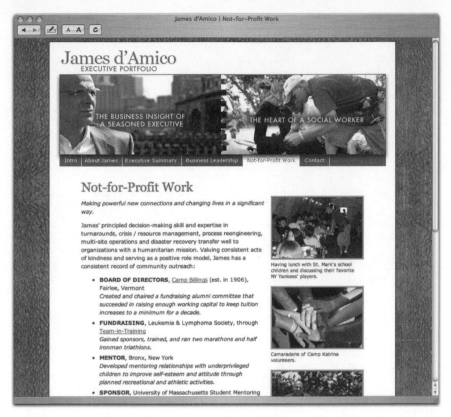

Figure 13.2   Using a Professional Photo on a Website

career services in five languages, understands this. The background texture of her website design features meaningful words in each of the languages in which she is fluent. For Patricia Moriarty, a specialist in technology for education, Brandego designed a circuit-board texture on a chalkboard specifically for her (see Figure 13.3). You can imagine this same pattern on the back of Patricia's business card, printed as a border on a correspondence card, and so forth.

Tagline

Your tagline is a short, often catchy phrase that communicates your unique promise of value. Examples of product taglines include

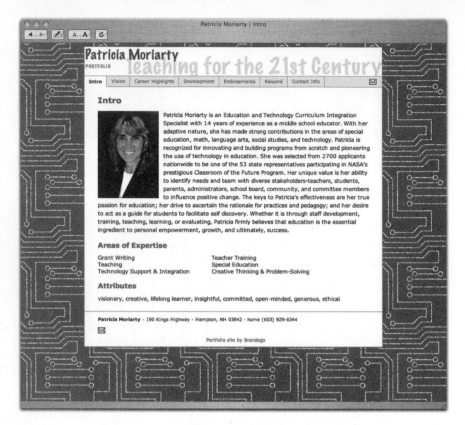

Figure 13.3   Using Background Texture to Communicate Your Brand

L'Oreal's "Because I'm Worth It" and Pepsi's "Generation Next." You can think of your tagline as a more marketing-oriented version of your brand statement. Taglines are often represented graphically in website designs, stationery, and other career-marketing tools.

When William was working as a brand manager at Lotus, he expressed his passion for branding, and in particular for the Lotus brand, with a tagline in his e-mail signature, "What have you done for the brand today?" When he founded Reach, that same tagline evolved—becoming "What have you done for YOUR brand today?"

Logo

If you have, or are planning to have, your own business or consulting practice, you will need a logo—an icon, graphic device, or type treatment expressing your brand. Not all logos consist of graphics. Indeed, many corporate logos—such as those for IBM, Google, and Jell-O—consist solely of stylized type. Figure 13.4 shows examples of graphical and stylized type logos.

Other Brand-Identity Elements

If appropriate for your brand, also consider using special effects—such as Flash animation, embossing, or metallics—in your online or printed career-marketing materials to convey one or more of your attributes. For example, the boxes shown on Jell-O's home page jiggle when site visitors move their cursor over the images.

Music or sound can constitute another effective element in your brand-identity system. Your presentations, podcasts, and website greeting could always begin and end with the same music, for example. What sound comes to mind when you think of Intel? William makes good use of audio in his monthly personal branding

Figure 13.4   Logo Types

quick tips (http://www.reachcc.com/link/WilliamArrudaQuickTip) by adding a refined, produced quality to them. He has also selected some snappy music to convey the notion of "quick."

How do you decide which elements to include in your brand-identity system? Complete the exercise in the *Career Distinction Workbook* to begin generating ideas.

Implementing Your Brand-Identity System

All of your career-marketing communications should be stamped with your brand identity (see Figure 13.5). These communications may include:

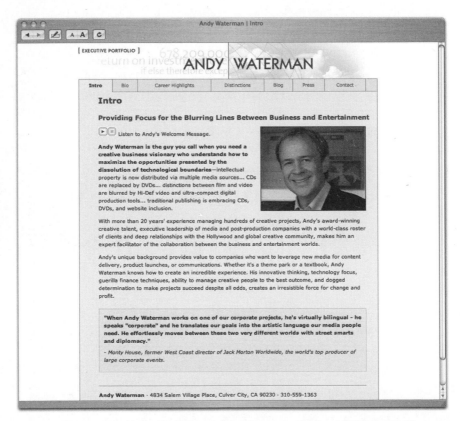

Figure 13.5 Andy Waterman's Personal Brand-Identity System

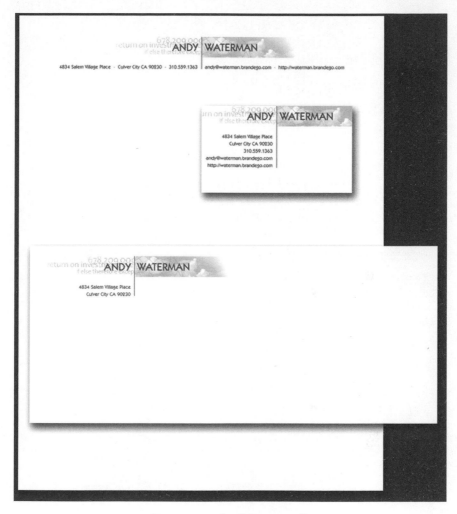

Figure 13.5 *(Continued)*

- Personal business cards for networking that include a link to your Web portfolio or blog.
- Letterhead, correspondence cards, envelopes, and labels.
- Thank-you notes.
- Custom PowerPoint or Keynote presentation template.

- Photo or logo postage stamps (as allowed in your country; personalized postage stamps are available in the United States at http://photo.stamps.com).
- Voicemail greetings.
- E-mail templates.
- Website.

> **Tip:** Once you have painstakingly selected each element (fonts, colors, logo, etc.) of your brand identity system, create a usage guide that you can refer to each time you create new marketing materials.

Creating your brand-identity system is just one part of Step 3: Exude—Managing Your Brand Environment. You must also strengthen your relationships with members of your brand community. The next chapter turns to this subject.

Chapter 14

Increase Your Career Karma

In this chapter, you will learn:

- To appreciate career karma—the phenomenon by which the more you give to others, the more you get in return
- Ways to strengthen relationships with members of your brand community
- The key to effective networking
- The widespread benefits of giving back to society

Professional success does not happen in a vacuum. Executives, managers, and entrepreneurs who achieve their career goals make a concerted, ongoing effort to connect with—*and support*—the members of their brand communities. Your professional network—those members of your brand community with whom you connect directly—is a vital element in your brand environment. When the members of your network respect you and understand your brand, they give you their support as you advance your career. They also extend your brand for you—by carrying your message to additional people on your behalf. While investing in the stock market these days doesn't always guarantee a profit, investing in your contacts yields a very high return: a rewarding career. As you probably know, word-of-mouth marketing is one of the best branding tools. And when you please your network members, you give them something they want to talk about with others.

You've probably heard the statistic that nearly two-thirds of all jobs are found through networking. Yet many people don't devote ongoing, steady effort to building and maintaining their network of contacts. At the same time, the need for networking has never been greater as executives increasingly face a revolving door in the form of ever-shorter tenures. Combine the fact that most jobs are found through networking with this trend of decreasing tenure, and we're certain you can appreciate the importance of investing in your social capital. As with any investment, this one requires focus and commitment. Take your eye off the stock market at any time, and you risk losing some of your hard-earned cash. It's the same with networking. To maximize your social capital, you must forge new relationships while also maintaining your existing attachments. The story that follows illustrates the value of networking.

FRANK NOVO, CUSTOMER SERVICE DIRECTOR

Frank Novo is the consummate networker. It's in his DNA. He not only builds relationships as a matter of course; he also maintains them. He is one of the only people in the Somerset High School class of '79 to attend *all* of the reunions. His gift for forging strong relationships came through clearly as a strength in his 360°Reach analysis. And that strength helped him when he found himself looking for a job after 15 years with NCR. His department at NCR was sold off to another company, and the management team told everyone to look for new jobs. Frank put the word out to his vast and solid network of contacts. A month before his last day at NCR, he had three job offers in hand.

You have to develop a Rolodex obsession, building and deliberately managing an ever-growing network of professional contacts.

　　　　　　　　　　　—Tom Peters, management guru

Career Karma: Give to Get

Although you need your professional contacts to support *your* success, building a valuable network hinges on *giving*—not taking. The more you give to your network members, the more they will be there for you when you most need them.

When someone comes to me for advice on how to build a network because they need a job now, I tell them it's useless. People can tell the difference between desperation and an earnest attempt to create a relationship.

　　　　　　　—Keith Ferrazzi, author of the bestselling
　　　　　　　　　networking book *Never Eat Alone* and one
　　　　　　　　　　of the world's most connected individuals

Networking is not about making superficial contacts just to meet your immediate need. It's about cultivating relationships. And like all relationships, the most successful networking bonds benefit both parties. When you approach networking from the perspective of giving, you make small but regular deposits in your social capital account, steadily increasing its value. You treat *all* members of your brand community generously—for example, by giving them new-customer leads, pointing them to resources that they might find useful, and helping them solve business problems. And the more you give, the more you get. Why? In the new world of work, what goes around comes around. In a word, it's all about karma.

Never has this concept of career karma been more crucial. In today's workplace, we each must fend for ourselves—making it essential that we support one another. By staying connected to others, you increase the exchange of advice, contacts, wisdom, and moral support circulating out there in the world.

> *I absolutely believe in the power of giving back. My own experience about all the blessings I've had in my life is that the more I give away, the more that comes back. That is the way life works, and that is the way energy works.*
>
> —Ken Blanchard, leadership author

In your professional life, you've probably met "takers." These individuals are always willing to ask for things but prove quite stingy when it comes to giving. They view the world through a lens of scarcity, not abundance. And as you might expect, they don't get as far in their professional *or* personal lives as people who demonstrate a more generous spirit. Perhaps you've been contacted by a long-lost member of your network only because she was now seeking a job. How did that make you feel?

If you view the world through a lens of abundance rather than paucity, you will find it easier to give to those around you, and you'll be much more likely to receive the support *you* need. Successful careerists live in a world of limitless possibilities, unending resources, and rich opportunities. Paul Copcutt, facilitator for the Reach Personal Branding Certification program, illustrates the power of giving to your network with this anecdote:

> I went to hear Keith Ferrazzi speak at the University of Toronto's Rotman business school. I learned of it from my contact there; I had spoken to their MBA alumni a few months earlier on personal branding. I broadcast the Keith Ferrazzi event to my 2,500

e-zine readers—about 10 percent of the 120 or so audience were people there directly from my e-zine notice.

I followed Keith's advice in his book about "bumping" the speaker before they go and then engaging them quickly to gain a follow-up. I took my copy of Keith's book, *Never Eat Alone*, and asked him to sign it "before he got famous" (a quote from the book about the speaker being mobbed afterward). He commented that I had obviously read the book. I said that William Arruda had recommended it last year and that it was my most referred and recommended book of the year. I then told Keith that I would like the opportunity to follow up with him to discuss how I can make *Never Eat Alone* the number-one networking book in Canada. He said, "Absolutely" and gave me his card with an invitation to call him.

As I walked away, someone behind me had taken my lead and asked for their book to be signed. I heard Keith ask the person for his thoughts on the book, and the man said, "I have the guy you were just talking with to thank for telling me about this book. I was unemployed at the time, and directly as a result of your book, I've now landed a job."

During Keith's talk (which was excellent), he referred to this person, Bob, and said how touched he was that his book had made such a difference. He then explained that Bob "has to thank this gentleman for even being here," and he pointed to me. He asked me to state my name and invited me to stand up. Then he said, "I talk on the subject of your brand, but as a direct result of Bob hearing about personal branding from Paul, he is now employed. So you should all take a moment to remember this face. And if you want to find out more about personal branding, this man has the program for you."

Needless to say, I had a steady line of people afterward queuing up to exchange business cards and express their interest in my program.

> *Your most precious, valued possessions and your greatest powers are invisible and intangible. No one can take them. You, and you alone, can give them. You will receive*

abundance for your giving. The more you give—the more you will have!

—W. Clement Stone, businessman and
advocate of positive mental attitude

Give without Being Asked

What's the ultimate gift? Giving to someone who hasn't asked for help. You enhance your social capital even more by recognizing that someone in your brand community has a need you can fill—and pitching in without being asked. Some people find it difficult to call on others for something they need. To give to these individuals, get to know them: The stronger your relationship and the deeper your knowledge of the other person, the more easily you can sense when he or she needs something—and proactively respond to that need. When you practice this kind of giving, you attain the highest level in the karma kingdom. The story that follows depicts one professional who excelled at giving without being asked.

MARY, EXECUTIVE ASSISTANT

Mary was the glue holding her organization's people together. Mary's personal brand attributes are empathy, compassion, collaboration, confidence, and intuition. She could tell when someone was not himself or herself, and would immediately offer her support—simply lending an ear or providing words of encouragement. She got others to give also. One day, William heard her whispering to a colleague outside his office, "Steven seems stressed today. If you have some time to share a kind word or a joke with him, I'm sure he'll appreciate it."

Mary's empathy and team spirit kept the organization functioning. Her bottomless store of generosity enabled the people around her to give their best on the job and draw maximum satisfaction from their work. And she was loved by all around her. When her position was eliminated after a reorganization, managers from throughout the company reached out to offer her a position on their team.

Starting with the Next Cubicle

Do you send e-mails or instant messages to people who work in the next office? If you do, you're missing one of the best opportunities to network: face-to-face exchanges with people in your organization. Some business professionals mistakenly assume that networking means cultivating relationships only with *external* contacts. But restricting your networking attempts to individuals outside your organization can damage your relationships with internal constituents. The following story shows how.

MARIA, DIRECTOR, PRODUCT MANAGEMENT

For Maria's colleagues and employees, one word came to mind when they thought about her: focused. Maria locked herself in her office every day and toiled over her e-mails and reports. She emerged only to take the necessary bathroom break. She worked hard in order to make things easier on her staff, but they saw it differently. Her 360°Reach self-evaluation featured attributes like compassion, empathy, and caring. Yet, feedback from peers and employees seemed to be describing someone else entirely—a person who was self-centered, independent, and thoughtless.

Maria was shocked when she saw the feedback, especially because it didn't match what her manager, friends, and family said about her. When she thought about it though, she understood what caused the disparity. She was so intent on getting her work done that she hadn't taken time to nurture relationships with her team members and colleagues. She reserved socializing and chit-chat for networking meetings, dinners with family and friends, and so forth. Maria realized that by locking herself in her office and not saying a word, she was actually—and unwittingly— sending the message that she didn't care about the people around her. And that message wasn't helping her advance her career. Although already fairly senior, she would need to demonstrate her ability to lead and support her team in order to further her career aspirations. This realization empowered Maria to make changes to how she worked. She now lunches in the cafeteria every day and spends a little more time around the water cooler as well.

Participating in professional associations and external activities (the outer rings of your brand community), as well as making connections through virtual networks such as LinkedIn (refer back to Chapter 11), can be valuable activities. But as Maria's story demonstrates, you can generate even more social capital by connecting with your colleagues *inside* the walls of your company. Why? Since the average tenure of an executive position is waning, your colleagues at your current organization may well be working somewhere else soon. And anytime one of your network members moves to a new employer, you gain fresh contacts in those other companies as well as opportunities to incorporate newcomers at your existing company into your professional network. Thus, investing in your internal network pays double returns. Try that with the stock market.

Finally, the best-connected executives and managers do a little networking each day—forging new relationships while also strengthening bonds with their existing contacts. They make networking a daily routine, like brushing their teeth. To increase the value of your social capital, adopt the same approach. Include in your daily "to do" lists activities that will help you make new contacts and enhance existing ones. Networking, just like other personal branding activities, is something you do "ongoingly."

This book is powerful proof of the value of networking. Our book proposal was referred to our editor, Laurie Harting, via a network contact—L. Michelle Tullier (a networking expert who wrote a book on the topic). Kirsten and Michelle had met many years ago when Michelle taught a course at NYU in career counseling that Kirsten took, and they had remained in touch. Kirsten introduced William to Michelle at the Career Masters Institute Conference in Denver where William delivered the keynote presentation. When we were looking for guest experts for our Reach Branding Club teleseminars, we asked Michelle to share some of her networking wisdom, and she kindly agreed. Michelle then proactively introduced us to an outplacement company that was interested in including executive branding in their offerings. In August of 2006, we asked Michelle if she could introduce us to her editor at John Wiley & Sons. She immediately responded to our request, giving us contact information and encouraging us to use her name. We e-mailed Michelle's editor who quickly referred us to the right editor at Wiley for our book. Just three weeks later, after a few conference calls and e-mails, we were negotiating the contract. Without Michelle's referral, it could have taken us much longer to secure a publisher with the international reach that we desired.

Tip: When you meet someone new, go through your mental Rolodex identifying people you know who would be valuable contacts for this new acquaintance.

The Dual Advantages of Social Capital

Your social capital not only helps you find a job, it enables you to *do* your job. As an executive or manager, you bring a major asset to your employer: your collection of contacts. The more people you know, the more easily you find the resources necessary to manage your job responsibilities. For example, if you're the head of product development and your team needs to find a new designer, you may know someone who will fit the bill. Or if you're the IT director and your department is thinking about adopting a new customer relationship management system, you probably know numerous people who can lend their opinions on the various systems you're evaluating. Even though networking isn't listed in your job description, consider it one of your most important responsibilities.

People with winning personal brands know that the lone-ranger approach to career management doesn't work. If you watch *The Apprentice*, you may have noticed that Donald Trump is connected to a host of individuals who help him succeed. Other major brands—Jack Welch, Richard Branson, Bill Gates, Oprah—all work the same way. And if you look closely at the executives whom you know and respect most, you will probably see that they, too, regularly draw on an immense store of social capital—a wealth of solid, mutually beneficial relationships with colleagues, clients, business partners, former supervisors, mentors, and so forth.

Demonstrating Your Personal Social Responsibility

One effective strategy for building your network is through giving back to society. Every major corporation does this through its corporate social responsibility initiatives. For example, British Petroleum works to create a cleaner environment, American Express contributes to efforts aimed at ending world hunger, and Avon supports breast-cancer awareness. Companies that genuinely and wholeheartedly embrace an important social cause gain an edge over rivals claiming that "it's not our job to worry about social problems." Socially responsible organizations increase their visibility, attract loyal customers, and enable their employees to feel the satisfaction that comes with contributing to something larger than themselves and their company.

> **Tip:** Revisit the values and passions exercises you
> completed in the *Career Distinction Workbook*
> (www.careerdistinction.com/workbook) to identify
> **causes you can support that link to your values and passions.**

Demonstrating *personal* social responsibility can give you advantages, too—including burnishing your personal brand and thereby further distinguishing you from competitors. For example, renowned U.K. chef, Jamie Oliver, is working to reduce obesity by making school lunches more healthful. Bill and Melinda Gates have created a foundation devoted to make education available to everyone around the globe. And Madonna is feeding and educating orphans in Malawi, Africa.

When you support a cause you care about, you have to trust that your generosity will come back to you—but without expecting the return to take any specific form. Think of personal social responsibility as a strategic way of managing your career, rather than a tactical plan that will generate specific outcomes. The results will be positive, but you cannot—nor should you try to—predict exactly what shape they will take. When Bob Geldof founded Band Aid to help ease poverty and starvation in Africa, he probably wasn't thinking, "Hmmm, if I start this organization, then I'll be knighted by the queen and nominated for a Nobel Peace Prize." Instead, he likely started Band Aid with the intention of giving wholeheartedly to a cause he felt passionate about.

> *I don't think you ever stop giving. I really don't. I think*
> *it's an ongoing process. And it's not just about being able*
> *to write a check. It's being able to touch somebody's life.*
>
> —Oprah Winfrey, Emmy award winning
> talk show host, philanthropist, and actor

You don't need a Swiss bank account to do your part in easing society's ills. *All* strong personal brands contribute to the world at large in some way. (In fact, you can think of "the world" as making up the outermost ring in your brand community.) Doing well usually puts you in an even better position to do good. Aiding others benefits you personally, helps society overall, and enhances your brand. It enables you to extend your professional network and sharpen your skills. It also makes you more interesting as an employee or as a candidate for a new job. When you champion a cause, you do great things for your career *and* for your spirit while you're making the world a better place for others.

Here are just a few of the benefits that come with demonstrating personal social responsibility:

- You meet others, expanding your network.
- You reinforce and augment your expertise.
- You broaden your perspective.
- You contribute to a passion.
- You increase your visibility.
- You connect with the larger world.
- You develop professionally by mastering new skills.
- You become a much more interesting and attractive professional or job candidate.
- You demonstrate leadership, communication, and project management skills.
- You help change the world for the better.

Remember: *All* your professional interactions collectively communicate your brand and thus determine your career destiny. Networking and demonstrating personal social responsibility count among the most powerful levers for benefiting yourself and those around you, as well as contribute to the career karma so essential to professional success. All this is vital to exuding—managing your brand environment. But the best brands do even more: They "evolve and resolve"—a topic we discuss in the concluding chapter.

Summary

Evolve and Resolve

In this chapter, you will learn:

- How to measure your brand's success
- How to ensure that your brand stays relevant
- How to keep branding at the forefront of your attention

By reading this book, using the 360°Reach personal brand assessment, and working on the exercises in the *Career Distinction Workbook,* you've taken those all-important first steps in the personal branding process. Now you know what you want from your career and what you must do to achieve your professional goals. But personal branding is not a one-time event. To stay on the path to success, you need to continually assess how your brand is performing and make adjustments as needed to continue advancing toward your professional goals.

As we noted in the beginning chapters, career management is something you should be doing every day. When you adopt this mindset, you gain control over your professional destiny, you deliver greater value to your employer or clients, and you move steadily toward your objectives. All strong brands remain self-aware and relevant so they can maintain career momentum.

> *As you begin to take action toward the fulfillment of your goals and dreams, you must realize that not every action will be perfect. Not every action will produce the desired result. Not every action will work. Making mistakes, getting it almost right, and experimenting to see what happens are all part of the process of eventually getting it right.*
>
> —Jack Canfield, author of
> *Chicken Soup for the Soul*

Assess Your Brand's Performance

You've unearthed your unique promise of value. You've identified communications tools to reach your target audience, and you've devised a plan for ensuring that your communications are clear, consistent, and constant (the three Cs of branding). You've also figured out how to shape your brand environment, including building and strengthening your professional network. But how will you know whether these efforts are paying off? You must regularly assess your brand's performance.

Only you can decide how to measure your brand's effectiveness. The key is establishing metrics up front, for example, is it:

- The size of your raise?
- Your satisfaction with your work/nonwork balance?
- The speed at which you advance in your career?
- The performance appraisal you receive at the end of the year?
- Your progress against a specific set of professional goals?
- The number of people who comment on your blog or subscribe to your newsletter?

- The quantity of your LinkedIn contacts?
- The number of speaking gigs you schedule each year?

No matter which metrics you select, make sure you check your brand's performance against those metrics at least once a year. Every major corporation performs brand measurement as a matter of course. Some companies spend hundreds of thousands of dollars on research to understand consumer perceptions of their brands, gauge brand awareness, and evaluate the strength of emotional and rational brand attributes. You must conduct similar research on your own brand's performance against the metrics you've chosen (of course, with a more modest budget!). Refer to the exercise in the *Career Distinction Workbook* for support in determining metrics.

Tip: Review your goals every Friday afternoon (remember, you documented them and posted them where you would see them), and ask yourself if your weekly accomplishments have helped you move toward those goals.

Ask for Feedback

Identify trusted colleagues, superiors, clients, and peers inside and outside your organization who can provide honest feedback on your brand. Ask them, "How am I doing?" at different stages of your relationship with them; you'll gain valuable insights. Get as much *input* as you can, to make your brand's *output* as strong as possible. Document this input in the associated exercise in the *Career Distinction Workbook* so you can refer to it as needed. When you receive this input, look at it through the lens of what will help you achieve your goals. Which pieces of feedback are most valuable to your success? How can you integrate this feedback into your career management strategy?

Here are some ways to gather feedback:

- *Look at your performance evaluations with a new set of eyes.* What's your manager saying about your brand as he or she comments on your achievements and improvement areas?
- *Solicit feedback after presentations.* If you deliver a speech or presentation for a professional organization, provide feedback forms and ask for specific input. For example, in Chapter 5 we shared with you that William obtains feedback after every workshop he delivers by asking participants to come up to the flip charts and write down one brand attribute they would associate with him. He saves all of these to see how consistent they are. If inconsistencies creep in, then he knows that he is not consistently delivering on his brand promise and he must reevaluate all elements of his speaking activities (the presentation, handouts, performance, etc.).
- *Repeat your brand assessment.* In a year's time, complete another 360°Reach brand assessment. Then compare the results to the baseline assessment you just did. Is your brand becoming more consistent? Is there more congruence between how you perceive yourself and how others perceive you? Are you becoming known for what you want to be known for? If not, what changes might you make to achieve greater congruence and consistency between others' perceptions of you and your own perceptions of yourself?
- *Look to a mentor or coach.* Ask your mentor or coach to give you direct, honest, and regular feedback on how you're coming across in your communications and on-the-job behaviors. After all, that is part of his or her job description.

Help Your Brand Evolve

As things change around you, you'll want to constantly assess your brand and the value that it's bringing you. By paying daily attention to what is and what isn't rewarding about your career, you can adapt your efforts to make any needed midcourse corrections.

> *When you're finished changing, you're finished.*
> —Benjamin Franklin, inventor and statesman

To remain relevant to their target audiences, all strong brands evolve with the times. In the business world, these changes could come in the form of product-line extensions. For example, Nick Graham of Joe Boxer went from novelty neckties to underwear. You might also change the way you communicate your brand, such as publishing a project proposal on a website instead of on paper in order to reach a larger audience. In addition, you could augment your brand attributes as you progress in your career (much as Volvo has been adding the attribute "style" to "safety" in the design of its cars).

Kirsten's brand has evolved significantly since she began her branding journey in 2004. As she launched Brandego and Reach Branding Club, she realized that she had found her niche as a career-technology expert. Even though she had built this reputation within one professional association, she hadn't fully committed to it, nor was she expressing it consistently. When her original business didn't fit with her newly defined brand, she sold it. (Another reason for selling it was to keep her sanity: Having three companies at the same time was not enjoyable!) When Kirsten found that she could reach a wider audience through speaking, writing, and developing products and services, she began to spend more time working in these creative areas—which are much more in line with her talents and long-term goals.

As you track your progress toward your goals, ask yourself whether your brand still aligns with your goals and whether you've developed the right communications mix to make your brand visible and credible. You may also want to revisit the Step 1: Extract chapters in this book to see whether any of your responses have changed over time. If they have, then reexamine and update your brand statement and profile.

12 Ways to Maintain *Career Distinction*

In the new world of work, the only constant is change. Thus, you cannot stand still as everything around you evolves. But fine-tuning your brand doesn't mean losing your authenticity. In fact, it suggests quite the opposite. As your brand evolves, it becomes an even more accurate representation of who you are. No matter how your brand might change, your larger vision and long-term goals remain constant. Evolving your brand means thinking of new *ways* to deliver on your personal brand promise. And it means making changes to continue maintaining your career distinction. We leave you with the following 12 tips for ensuring that you stand out—always:

1. *Know yourself.* You can't stand out if you don't know who you are and what you want from life. People who stand out are self-aware. Think Oprah.
2. *Flaunt your quirks.* Standing out is about differentiating yourself. Don't hide what makes you different. Accentuate it.
3. *Maximize your strengths.* People who stand out are those who are "best" at something. Think Tiger Woods, Bill Gates, Lance Armstrong. Standing out is all about superlatives.
4. *Google yourself regularly.* Ego-surf frequently. Others are Googling you. You need to know and manage your online reputation. Remember: To some people, you *are* your Google results.
5. *Ask for feedback.* Realize that your reputation counts. Proactively seek feedback to understand how others perceive you.
6. *Be a connector.* Make sure people see you as the nucleus in every organization you're helping to grow.
7. *Think big.* Have big dreams, and be willing to take the steps needed to turn those dreams into reality.
8. *Keep refining.* Never be happy with how things are today. Be a lifelong learner, ambitious, and focused on your personal and professional growth.

9. *Define your own crowd*. Know as much as you can about your competitors so you can use your uniqueness to stand out.

10. *Give to your network*. Help members of your professional networks make new contacts, find valuable information, and identify new opportunities. The more you give to your network members, the more you get.

11. *Mark everything you do*. Put a piece of who you are into everything you do—every phone call, email, meeting, and personal interaction.

12. *Be a confident communicator*. Demonstrate your conviction, passion, and confidence in all your communications. People will not only notice you—they'll remember you long after you've delivered your message.

Appendix

We are delighted to present the Reach Certified Personal Brand Strategists that span the globe. To learn more about them, just Google their names:

The Americas

United States	Arkansas	JoAnn Nix
	California	Justine Arian
		Pat Barrett
		Nina Burokas
		Karen Fazio
		Char Geary
		Gerri Gordon
		Jana Hayes
		Cindy King
		Myriam-Rose Kohn
		Adam Leavitt
		Julie Maiz
		Lidia Pusnik
		Doreen Ramsey
		Sharon Stenger
		Ruth Villarreal
		Debbie Watson
		Katherine Zimmer
	Connecticut	Louise Garver
	Florida	Mark S. Grogan
		Beverly Harvey
		Cindy Kraft
		Claudine Vainrub Kupchik

Georgia	Walter Akana
	Jai Stone
Hawaii	Phyllis Horner
Illinois	Murray A. Mann
	Angela Orrico
Iowa	Marcy Johnson
Massachusetts	Jean Cummings
	Sherri Fisher
	Stacy Graiko
	Patricia Soldati
Minnesota	Nancy Branton
Missouri	Frank E. Rolfe
New Hampshire	Michelle Dumas
New Jersey	Winnie Anderson
	Rose Rybski
	Kathy Warwick
	Martin Weitzman
New Mexico	Richard Freedman
New York	Deb Dib
	Sally Robertson
	Phyllis Shabad
	Beth Stefani
North Carolina	Jacqui Brett
Oklahoma	Bonnie Kurka
Oregon	Stacey Lane
Pennsylvania	Carla Gauthier
	Casey Giovinco
	Charley Timmins
	Linda Yaffe
Texas	Maria Duron
	Edie Rische
Utah	Jason Alba
Washington	Kim Batson
	Mixie Kingman Eddy
Washington, DC	Abby Locke
Wisconsin	Carmen Croonquist

		Susan Guarneri
		Christine Jacobs
		Wendy Terwelp
Canada	Alberta	Deborah Reaburn
	Ontario	Harp Arora
		Martin Buckland
		Amy Casson
		Paul Copcutt
		Kaitlin Eckler
		Kathryn Ferguson
		Pamela Hill
		Ross Macpherson
		Erin Morehouse
	Quebec	Danielle Silverman
Bahamas		Stacia Williams

Asian Pacific

China		Marc Hong
	Hong Kong	Rosemarie Yau
Indonesia		Ivan Soeira
Malaysia		Nora Al Yahya
Singapore		Han Kok Kwang
		Chia Weng Lee

Europe, Middle East, and Africa

Egypt		Riham El-Hawary
France		Pascale Baumeister
		Michael Colemyn
		Beatrice Cuvelier
		Francine Grignon
		Elodie Le Gendre
		Eric Madier
		Bernadette Martin
		Severine Messier

France	Stéphanie Noel
	Nathalie Renard
	Odile Tourret
Ireland	Krishna De
Israel	Haya Hachamov
Italy	Megan Fitzgerald
Mauritius	J Darlene Lam Po Tang
	Tasneem Patel
Portugal	R. Miguel Coelho
Russia	Caroline Elias
South Africa	Andrew Clare
	Makhosazana Matsipa
	Matlankose Matsipa
Sweden	Frances Broman
United Kingdom	Tania Abdulezer
	Sinead Allan
	Sue Brettell
	Trevor Cousins
	Rob Cuesta
	Sharon Gaskin
	Martin Hogg
	Julie Dorman
	Maureen O'Grady
	Nancy Preston
	Dorothea Stuart
	Lily Yeboah
	Findlay Young

These professionals have either completed or are in the process of completing a rigorous and comprehensive 60-hour personal branding certification program. Learn more about how you can put Reach's leading personal branding methodology to work with your clients at www.reachcc.com/certification.

Index

About the Authors

WILLIAM ARRUDA is an executive coach, public speaker, and author. He combines his 20 years' corporate branding experience, passion for human potential, and avid pursuit of innovation to help professionals stand out and expand their success. He is the founder of Reach, the global leader in personal branding and cofounder of the Reach Branding Club. JPMorgan, Disney, Adobe, Microsoft, Warner Bros, British Telecom, Electronic Arts, and Starwood Hotels are just a few of the corporate clients for whom he's delivered presentations and workshops on the transformative power of personal branding. William has appeared on BBC TV, the Discovery Channel, and Fox News Live. A sought-after spokesperson on career advancement, he has been featured in and written for the *Wall Street Journal, Harvard Business Review, Time, Forbes,* and many other publications throughout the world. He holds a master's degree in education.

KIRSTEN DIXSON is an authority on building credible online identities for career success. She founded Brandego and is a partner in Reach. Kirsten is a contributor to more than 15 career books, serves on the board of The Career Management Alliance, appears nationally as a speaker, and is frequently quoted in articles about career-related technology. As one of the world's first Reach-Certified Personal Branding Strategists and a Certified Job and Career Transition Coach, she has successfully helped hundreds of professionals market themselves for new careers. Kirsten earned a BA degree from Vassar College and a Certificate in Adult Career Planning and Development from New York University.

Go to www.careerdistinction.com/workbook for access to the Brand Assessment tool and the workbook!

Dear Readers,

To access the *Career Distinction Workbook* and the 360°Reach Brand Assessment please go to **www.careerdistinction.com /workbook.** Once there, book purchasers will be able to download the workbook and register to get access to 360°Reach.

This tool is complimentary and as such customer support is limited. The authors reserve the right to limit the number of complimentary passwords for 360°Reach.